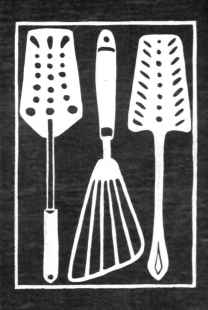

Rhubarb

jam

The
Auntie Em's Cookbook

A Musician's Guide
to Breakfast & Brunch
& Dessert!

By Theresa Wahl

Photography by David Kiang

PROSPECT
· PARK ·
BOOKS

Published by Prospect Park Books
969 S. Raymond Avenue
Pasadena, California 91105
www.prospectparkbooks.com

Distributed by Consortium Books Sales & Distribution
www.cbsd.com

Library of Congress Cataloging in Publication Data is on file with the Library of Congress.
The following is for reference only:

Wahl, Theresa
The Auntie Em's Cookbook: a musician's guide to breakfast & brunch / by Theresa Wahl — 1st ed.
     p. cm.
ISBN: 978-1-938849-26-8

1. Cooking, American. 2 Breakfast and brunch. 3. Dessert and baking. I. Title.

Edited by Colleen Dunn Bates
Recipes edited by Jenn Garbee
Assistant editor: Jennifer Bastien
Editorial & design assistant: Renee Nakagawa

Photographs by David Kiang
Photo styling by Amy Paliwoda
Props & surfaces provided by the Surface Library, thesurfacelibrary.com
Drawings & woodcuts by Annika Huston

Designed by Amy Inouye, Future Studio

First edition, first printing

Printed in China by Imago USA on sustainably produced, FSC-certified paper

THE FANS SPEAK

"Tenacious D loves Auntie Em's. Her delicious nutrients are always energizing and indie-fresh. Where does she find those unbelievable recipes? Somewhere over the rainbow?"
— JACK BLACK (of the D)

"I'm excited to finally be able to bring Terri Wahl's world home with me to recreate the inimitable Auntie Em's vibe at home. I'll throw on some '80s English punk on the stereo (Siouxsie & the Banshees "Kaleidoscope," perhaps), gather my friends and loved ones on my porch, and pogo around the kitchen while I cook up some of my fave cravings: Mabel's Short Stack, the best grits and eggs this side of the Mississippi, and that amazing coconut cake."
— KATE SCHELLENBACH, Luscious Jackson & Beastie Boys

"I like to go to the horse races, but I don't usually win with the horses, so afterward I go to Auntie Em's and drown my sorrows in a red velvet cupcake. It never fails me."
— RUSSELL MAEL, Sparks

"The first time I went to Auntie Em's, I knew this was my place. I love everything about it and could eat there every day. Of course, that means I'd be eating a red velvet cupcake every day, and I just can't have that."
— JOSH KLINGHOFFER, Red Hot Chili Peppers

"Nobody whips an electric guitar or shreds a frittata quite like Terri Wahl. She's a one-of-a-kind musician/chef who somehow manages to mashup contemporary California cooking with traditional comfort food and spin out something that's soulful and wonderful. Punk rock never tasted so good."
— MARK HASKELL SMITH,
author of *Heart of Dankness* and *Raw: A Love Story*

My Mom

This book is hugely dedicated to my mom, Christine Wright. She grew fruit and veggies in our backyard before it was cool. She composted before it was trendy. She was the original homesteader.

My mom cooked from scratch every night. She actually had warm homemade chocolate chip cookies and cold milk ready for my sister Lisa and me when we got home from school. She pickled, preserved, baked, and cooked, and she still does all that. It is her art form.

My mother helps me arrange flowers and produce for the weddings that Auntie Em's caters. She does all the gardening at the restaurant, and she cooks me a three-course dinner when I come over. Not super-fancy restaurant food, but the tasty comfort food she knows I love.

When I got the phone call that the Food Network wanted me to be on *Chopped*, Mom helped me practice—and she was more excited about me being on the show than I was. She was absolutely convinced that I'd beat anyone I had to cook against.

I got my first catering job—a dinner for sixty people—from my friend Joel, who produced music videos. I called my mom in a complete panic. What do I make? How do I transport it? Where do I shop? Calmly, she said she'd be there soon to help. That first catering job was such a success that I worked for the next five years on word of mouth alone.

My mom always tells my customers at Auntie Em's that I didn't get any of my talent from her. Nonsense. I got it all from her: passion, drive, creativity, and the love of good food. She shaped who I am today. So Mom, this book is for you.

What's Inside

FALL...90

Pear & Ginger Baked French Toast
Pumpkin Pancakes with Persimmons & Pecans
Fig, Blue Cheese & Prosciutto Tartine
Spicy Pimiento Cheese & Bacon Tartine
Andouille Sausage & Shrimp Scramble
Fennel, Tomato & Parmesan Salad with Poached Eggs
Fried Green Tomatoes & Eggs ♪ Braised Pork with Greens & Eggs
Roasted Mushroom Grits & Poached Eggs
Brussels Sprouts & Potato Hash with Poached Eggs
Herb-roasted Breakfast Potatoes
Double Garlic Greens ♪ Curried Chickpea Salad
Pear & Cranberry Compote

WINTER...118

Beet & Blood Orange Salad
Cranberry Beans with Black Kale & Red Chiles
Noah's Vegetarian Breakfast Torta ♪ Best Hot Chocolate
Wilted Spinach & Lentil Salad with Poached Eggs
Baked Eggs in Ham Baskets
Salmon & Fennel Scramble with Dill Crème Fraîche
Spicy Sausage & Cheddar Grits
Bacon, Onion Sprouts, Avocado & Egg Sandwich
Biscuits & Sausage Gravy
Swiss Chard Gratin

Rockin' the Kitchen

By Larry Hardy

I'll never forget the first time I met Terri Wahl. She was just sixteen, had a wild head of jet-black dyed hair, and was dressed head to toe in black (not a common look for conservative Anaheim in the early '80s). We were commiserating over the fact that both of our houses had been egged by the same girl the night before, and Terri said, "I'm gonna kick that bitch's ass." I knew right then and there that I was going to be good friends with this girl. If you would've told me back then that she'd end up being in an all-girl punk band, I'd have had no trouble believing it. I was, however, blown away the first time I tasted her cooking. When a twenty-year-old invites you to dinner, you're lucky if you get pasta with sauce from a jar. Terri served me a five-course dinner: a crab cream cheese dip, the most delicious sautéed vegetables I'd ever tasted, fish seasoned and baked to perfection, curried rice with peas, and an insane chocolate mousse. She made everything from scratch, and it was all out of this world, even the presentation and table settings. From then on, I always got giddy when I got an invitation for dinner at Terri's. I still get giddy.

The Red Aunts en route to Europe. L to R: Terri Wahl, Kerry Davis, Debi Martini, Leslie Ishino

I watched Terri forge both her musical and culinary careers with great pride and awe. She didn't let the fact that she had no musical experience stop her from forming a band. Within a few short years, the Red Aunts went from being a ragged, atonal opening act to a totally bulldozing art-punk band whose aggression was matched by its originality. By the time they called it a day in 1998, they had developed a large following, toured the United States and Europe extensively, signed to the world's biggest punk record label, and released five albums and a string of singles. They'd even been mentioned on an episode of *Roseanne*. Thankfully, Terri never allowed her obsession with good food to wane during her rock 'n' roll years. While on tour, she found the best restaurants, looked for regional cookbooks, and spent all those hours in the van reading *Martha Stewart Living*.

It made perfect sense that when the band came to an end, her second act would be cooking. She started her catering business in much the same way she started her band—she just jumped into the deep end and went for it. Except with this venture, her chops were already well honed, so she had immediate success.

I'm so glad that Terri has finally written a cookbook—actually, I think it's long overdue. I speak from firsthand experience when I say that Terri's cooking, much like the Red Aunts' music, totally rocks.

Larry Hardy owns the indie label In the Red Records.

Larry Hardy and Terri Wahl

From Punk Rock to Pulled Pork

I don't know where I'd be without my passion for food and music. Both have given me so much: a great band and a fantastic career in food.

My love for great food started as a kid, with my mother's gardening and cooking. But the story in this book really begins with my life as a musician. In the early '90s, my boyfriend was in a band, and so were my friends' boyfriends. We wanted a band, too, so Debi Martini and I started one. We got our friends Kerry Davis and Leslie Ishino to join us, and we became the Red Aunts—a band of four young chicks with huge attitudes and loud guitars. Most of us had never even played an instrument. Debi played bass and sang, Leslie played drums, and Kerry and I played guitar and sang. We were punk rock (mainly because we couldn't play), we were garage rock (mainly because we practiced in Debi's garage), and we were ragged (mainly because we couldn't really tune our guitars). We loved fashion and had a blast screaming our heads off about crushes, roller skating, our pets, broken hearts, food, and, well, boys. We weren't like the original punks, who sang about politics, hating the man, being poor, and doing drugs. We didn't really fit into the riot grrrl camp either, because we didn't hate boys...quite the contrary.

We talked a good friend of ours, Long Gone John, who had an indie label called Sympathy for the Record Industry, to put out a single on vinyl and our first CD. Then we got signed to the biggest indie punk-rock label, Epitaph, which was owned by my friend Brett Guerewitz. It was home to L7, Bad Religion, NOFX, Rancid, Pennywise, and the Offspring. The timing was lucky, because that's when the Offspring song "Keep Them Separated" broke on MTV. Then Rancid broke, and they became huge. Brett believed in taking the revenue from the "big bands" and investing it into what he called "the baby bands"—like us. He sent us on tour, so we could build a bigger fan base. We were in the right place at the right time, and it worked. The Red Aunts toured the United States many times and Europe once, and we released five albums.

In the Red Aunts van, instead of trashy magazines we had stacks of cookbooks and food magazines. In the early days, before we had a driver, we'd take turns driving while the other girls read cookbooks and talked about recipes we were going to make. It was all food all the time. In every town, we sought out the cafés and markets that represented the local food and culture. In Baltimore we'd head to the Lexington Market for live crawfish and

crabs. In Seattle it was Pike Place Market, always packed with people and fish. On our way to Oregon, we'd always eat at a little bakery called Heaven on Earth where you could get homemade blueberry pie and sticky buns the size of your head. At Mary Mac's Tea Room in Atlanta, Georgia, we'd dine on fried chicken, macaroni and cheese, collards, and sweet tea. In the middle of the country, we'd stop for breakfast at the Waffle House, where you could order hash browns smothered, covered, chunked, diced, peppered, capped, topped, or "countried"—which meant with sautéed onions, cheese, ham, tomatoes, jalapeños, mushrooms, chili, and gravy. I'd never heard of such a thing. Great hangover food! In Texas we'd stop at roadside stands for frozen ice pops made out of pickle juice: Pickle Sickles. New Orleans, of course, was a major destination for us: the best oysters I have ever had, crazy good gumbo, and a fried oyster po' boy that I will never forget, served at a corner market that a local told us about.

Auntie Em's Is Born

After a decade of touring and eating beautiful food around the world, I knew it was time for a new career: to build a life around making people happy by cooking for them. My friend Joel Tabbush got me a catering job on a video shoot. That led to jobs catering music videos, photo shoots, commercial shoots, and indie movies, all by word of mouth. I fed Cindy Crawford, Snoop Dogg, Alec Baldwin, Green Day, Jennifer Lopez, Rihanna, Busta Rhymes, Britney Spears, Tom Petty, Thom York, Katherine Heigl, Kool Keith, Lionel Ritchie, Elton John, Dr. Phil, and many more. For five years, I did it all out of my little rental house, where I had industrial shelving, multiple fridges, and a big, fat, fancy oven. Then one morning the health department showed up and was less than thrilled to see my operation. So I moved it to a tiny storefront in a quiet part of Eagle Rock, in northeast Los Angeles, near Occidental College. There was a little space in front where I could fit a few tables, so I opened a breakfast and lunch café.

I had a clear vision of what I wanted: a homey place that focused on American comfort food, where I could play cool music, work with my friends, and serve decadent desserts and a great breakfast. I wanted to serve hot soups with grilled-cheese sandwiches on cold days. I wanted to use as much organic, local produce as possible and make everything from scratch. I wanted a restaurant for the neighborhood—a place that truly cared about what it was feeding the professors on their lunch breaks, the college kids grabbing a piece of pie with friends, the tired parents stopping for breakfast after dropping off the kids at

The Red Aunts on the road. L to R: Terri Wahl, Kerry Davis, Debi Matini, Leslie Ishino

preschool. And finally, I wanted to create a work environment that my employees actually enjoyed being in.

From the beginning, I had this vision of making huge cupcakes that two people could split. (This was before the whole cupcake craze.) We became famous for our red velvet cupcakes, making hundreds of them a week at first, and then thousands. Our amazing bakers at the time, MaryEllen Mason and Michael Sullivan, had to completely rework the recipe to accommodate such huge batches. While they worked on the baking, I worked on my true love, the breakfast, brunch, and lunch dishes.

Auntie Em's grew. I rented the storefront next door and broke through the wall to double our size. We made the little waiting area into a gourmet marketplace. I worked really hard to find local artisans, and now we carry their preserves, cheeses, candy, kitchen items, and cookbooks.

I shopped the farmers' markets from day one, loading up my car to the roof to get the restaurant through the weekend. A chef friend, Fred Eric, introduced me to the farmers who supplied his restaurant, and I struck up relationships with farmers at the weekly markets. At first, my motivation was purely taste. When you buy a tomato that was picked the day before, it just tastes better. All the other good things about buying organic, local produce were bonuses. I'm happy to see that it's getting easier for home cooks to find quality organic produce, thanks to more farmers' markets and specialty markets.

A fellow restaurateur once told me that I could save so much money if I just bought my ketchup from the restaurant supply instead of making it in-house. But I didn't want to be in this business if that's what I had to do to succeed. It's never been about making money. It's about the meal we put in front of a customer, and the food we make for someone's wedding or birthday party. I would rather make less money serving better-tasting handmade food than cut corners. I hope to inspire you to do the same at home.

SHARING TIME

After eleven years running Auntie Em's Kitchen, and many more catering, it's time to share my very favorite breakfast, brunch, and dessert recipes. I've organized them around the seasons, because that's how I cook. Our blackboard menu showcases what's fresh, what's in season, what's really delicious that day. So there's a salad of peaches and garden greens in summer; baked eggs with kale and potatoes in winter; a frittata with asparagus and young purple onions in spring; and pear and ginger french toast in fall. Summer runs long here in California, but I never forget to set aside time in September to put up preserves with the late-summer produce, so there's a chapter in this book to encourage you to try preserving—and even make the same ketchup we make at Auntie Em's.

Finally, no matter the season, there are the desserts and breakfast pastries, from the red velvet cupcake that made us famous, to elaborate cakes for special occasions, to homey bars, hand pies, and cinnamon rolls. My bakers and I have spent years perfecting our baked goods, and we're happy now to share the recipes with you.

Instead of pairing wines with each recipe, I pair them with my favorite songs to listen to while I'm cooking. Yes, more than eighty favorite songs. Can you imagine how fun it was to build that playlist? Sharing my favorite recipes *and* finding the perfect songs to cook them by... I love my life!

Follow Terri on Instagram at Terriwahl666 or at facebook.com/auntieems

The Red Aunts, rippin' it

SPRING

SPRING RECIPES

English Pea, Asparagus & Edamame Salad

Arugula Salad with Strawberries & Goat Cheese

Garden Lettuces & Herbs
with the Perfect Poached Egg

Roasted Asparagus & Purple Spring Onion Frittata

Bread Pudding with Bacon & Herbs

Crab Cakes & Eggs
with Chipotle Aioli & Cilantro Pesto

Artichoke Baked Eggs

Crabby Deviled Eggs

Vegetarian Red Flannel Hash

Scalloped New Potatoes with Aged Cheddar

Asparagus with Gremolata

Rhubarb Compote

Indian Spiced Roasted Carrots

WHAT'S IN SEASON IN SPRING?

Artichokes	Kohlrabi
Arugula	Kumquats
Asparagus	Leeks
Beets	Morels
Carrots	New potatoes
Chard	Parsley
Cherries	Pea greens
Fava beans	Peas
Fennel	Radishes
Green garlic	Rhubarb
Green onions	Spinach
Kiwis	Strawberries

Spring Greens & Guitar Strings

Spring is my favorite time of year in my garden. The vegetables and fruit are so delicate: soft spring lettuces, slightly peppery chives, small strawberries that first taste so sweet and then end with a hint of tartness. I also plant sprouting broccoli, broccoflower, kale, French radishes, arugula, and Swiss chard. I like cutting the kale and chard when they're very young and using them raw in salads.

Springtime is also when the baby chicks arrive: tiny, peeping little fuzzballs. My chickens have a big coop in the backyard, under a tree. I usually have five to ten chickens, all hens of course (roosters are too loud for the city!), and they each lay an egg a day. Once you get your flock going, chickens are very easy to take care of: just ten minutes in the morning to feed them, give them fresh water, and collect their eggs. The only challenge is predators. I live at the bottom of a hillside in L.A. and am lucky to have a big yard. The first year I had chickens, I lost more than half of them to coyotes, red-tailed hawks, possums, and raccoons. I actually watched a hawk swoop down and pinch off my favorite teenage hen. I now have trenches lined with chicken wire so critters can't dig under the coop, and netting above the run so birds can't get them.

I use a lot of the vegetable scraps from the restaurant to feed the girls, as well as scraps from my home kitchen. The compost pile in their run gets stacked with old straw from the coop, coffee grounds, chicken poop, and spent plants from the garden. This gets mixed into the plant beds in my yard. It's a sustainable system, and it brings me both joy and delicious food.

I'm always so excited when spring rolls around. It's the first time in the year that I can have friends over for dinner in the garden—and to blast some music while we're at it. There's nothing I love more than sitting in my backyard with my friends, eating a wonderful meal and listening to great music.

English Pea, Asparagus & Edamame Salad

This salad is the essence of spring. Crisp, delicate peas, the tang of lemon, and the rich saltiness of parmesan make it the perfect side salad for a brunch menu.

Serves 4 as a side dish

1 cup English peas, shelled
1 cup edamame, shelled
1 cup asparagus (about 1/2 bunch) cut in 1/2-inch pieces, tough root ends trimmed
2 green onions, white and tender green stems only, minced
1 teaspoon minced garlic
3 tablespoons extra-virgin olive oil
Zest of 1 lemon
Juice of 1/2 lemon
1/2 cup shaved good parmesan, preferably Parmigiano Reggiano
Sea salt and freshly ground pepper

Prepare a large bowl of ice water and set aside.

Fill a medium saucepan halfway with water, add a pinch of salt, and bring to a boil. Add peas and cook until they are bright green, about 2 minutes. Working quickly, transfer with a slotted spoon to bowl of ice water to stop the cooking process. Repeat with edamame and asparagus, cooking until bright green and adding them to the same bowl of ice water. Drain vegetables through a strainer and transfer to a medium bowl.

Gently fold green onions, garlic, olive oil, lemon zest and juice, and parmesan into vegetables. Season with salt and pepper to taste. Serve at room temperature or chilled.

Song: Tive Razao, Seu Jorge

Arugula Salad
with Strawberries & Goat Cheese

This is a great salad for strawberry season; other times of the year, I use peaches, plums, or apples, depending on what's in season. The arugula is spicy and peppery, which balances perfectly with the sweet berries and creamy, tangy goat cheese.

Serves 4

1 clove garlic, minced
2 tablespoons balsamic vinegar
Sea salt and freshly ground pepper
4 tablespoons extra-virgin olive oil
8 loosely packed cups baby arugula
16 ounces strawberries, sliced (about 3 cups)
1/2 cup sliced almonds, toasted
6 ounces goat cheese, crumbled

In a small bowl, whisk together garlic, vinegar, pinch of salt, and a couple of grinds of pepper. While whisking, slowly drizzle in olive oil until emulsified, about 30 seconds.

Place arugula, strawberries, and almonds in a large bowl. Add balsamic vinaigrette and toss gently. Sprinkle with goat cheese and season with salt and pepper to taste. Serve immediately.

GARDEN LETTUCES & HERBS WITH THE PERFECT POACHED EGG

I make this dish for breakfast at least three times a week in the spring, using lettuces and herbs from my garden. You can also get delicate, tasty lettuces from farmers' markets and quality grocery stores. My chickens lay me beautiful little eggs that make this dish extra tasty. If you use store-bought eggs, make sure they are very fresh. The fresher the eggs, the easier they are to poach. Since it's best to eat poached eggs the moment they are ready, I always assemble the salad first.

Serves 4

Song: Beautiful Gardens, The Cramps

3 tablespoons apple cider vinegar
Sea salt
8 cups assorted lettuces, such as butter, little gem, mizuna, oak leaf,
   and/or watercress—whatever you have
1 cup assorted soft herbs, such as cilantro, flat-leaf parsley, dill, arugula, and/or basil
Juice of 1/2 lemon
2 tablespoons extra-virgin olive oil
Freshly ground pepper
4 very fresh eggs

Fill a wide, deep saucepan with about 4 inches water. Add vinegar and a pinch of salt and bring to a boil. Reduce heat so water remains at a gentle boil.

In a medium bowl, combine lettuces and herbs and toss gently. Add lemon juice and olive oil and toss again gently. Add salt and pepper to taste and arrange greens on 4 plates. Set aside.

Break 1 egg at a time into a small ramekin and tip egg into the water. Immediately repeat with remaining 3 eggs. Poach about 1 1/2 minutes for runny yolks, a bit more if you like firmer eggs. Lift out first egg with a slotted spoon and gently press the outside edge to make sure it is cooked to your liking. If so, rest spoon on a paper towel for a few seconds to drain excess water and place egg atop a salad. Repeat with remaining eggs. Finish each salad with a pinch of salt and a grind of pepper. Serve immediately.

ROASTED ASPARAGUS &
PURPLE SPRING ONION FRITTATA

Spring onions with their long, green stalks are beautiful in a frittata. Baby purple onions are my favorite and also look really cool, but you can use white onions. Make sure the heads are on the small side, not much bigger than your pinkie finger.

Song: The Day My Baby Gave Me a Surprise, Devo

Serves 2

1 bunch asparagus, root ends trimmed

1/4 cup extra-virgin olive oil, divided

1 teaspoon sea salt, divided

1 teaspoon freshly ground pepper, divided

1 tablespoon herbes de Provence, divided

2 cloves garlic, chopped

4 purple spring onions or green onions

1 medium yellow onion, finely chopped

6 large eggs

1/4 cup heavy cream

1/4 cup finely chopped flat-leaf parsley

Preheat oven to 450° and line 2 baking sheets with foil.

Cut asparagus into 1-inch pieces on the bias. Place in a medium mixing bowl and toss with 1 teaspoon olive oil, 1/4 teaspoon salt, 1/4 teaspoon pepper, 1 1/2 teaspoons herbes de Provence, and garlic. Distribute asparagus evenly on one baking sheet. Slice spring onions in half lengthwise, trim any brown, discolored ends from the stalks, and cut into 1-inch pieces. In same mixing bowl, toss onions with 2 teaspoons olive oil, 1/4 teaspoon salt, 1/2 teaspoon pepper, and remaining 1 1/2 teaspoons herbes de Provence. Distribute onions evenly on remaining baking sheet. Place baking sheets in oven and roast until vegetables begin to look crispy and golden brown on their edges, about 8 minutes. Remove and let cool for 5 minutes. Reduce heat to 350°.

Heat remaining 3 tablespoons olive oil in a 10-inch, nonstick skillet over medium heat. Add yellow onion and sauté until soft and translucent, about 7 minutes. Add asparagus and spring onion mixture and stir to combine. Remove from heat.

In the same mixing bowl, whisk eggs, cream, parsley, remaining 1/2 teaspoon salt, and remaining 1/4 teaspoon pepper until frothy. Pour egg mixture over vegetables in skillet. Bake until center is set, about 12 minutes. Let cool for 5 minutes. Cut into wedges and serve.

BREAD PUDDING WITH BACON & HERBS

We use a lot of bread at the restaurant, so we're always inventing new recipes to make good use of the day-old stuff. I like thinly sliced, country-style white bread, but you can use any leftover bread that is good quality. We always serve variations of this make-ahead recipe on the weekends. Pair it with fresh seasonal fruit or a small salad with olive oil and lemon to complement the richness of the bread pudding.

Serves 6 to 8

10 slices applewood-smoked bacon

3 tablespoons unsalted butter, softened

4 tablespoons finely chopped chives

4 tablespoons finely chopped basil

3 tablespoons finely chopped parsley

3 tablespoons finely chopped oregano

1 cup grated good cheddar
  (such as Hook's or Cabot Clothbound)

1 cup grated Gruyère cheese,
  plus 3 tablespoons for garnish

9 to 10 slices good-quality stale white
  bread, or any other bread, crusts
  trimmed and reserved for another use

2 teaspoons sea salt, divided

2 teaspoons freshly ground pepper, divided

10 large eggs

3 cups heavy cream

2 cups milk

1/2 teaspoon ground nutmeg

1/2 teaspoon cayenne pepper

Fry bacon in a large skillet over medium heat until crisp, about 4 to 5 minutes. Cut into 2-inch pieces and set aside on a paper towel to drain fat.

Rub a medium baking dish (about 10 1/2″ × 7″ or 1-quart gratin dish) with softened butter. In a medium bowl, mix together chives, basil, parsley, oregano, bacon, cheddar, and Gruyère. Line baking dish with a layer of bread (about 3 slices), trimming to fit if needed. Season bread with 1 teaspoon each salt and pepper. Scatter half of the bacon-cheese mixture over the bread. Repeat with a layer of bread and the remaining half of the bacon-cheese mixture. Finish with a layer of bread.

In a medium bowl, beat eggs with cream and milk. Season with 1 teaspoon each salt and pepper, nutmeg, and cayenne, and mix well. Pour egg mixture over bread. Sprinkle remaining 3 tablespoons Gruyère on top and cover with plastic wrap. Let sit in refrigerator for 24 hours.

Preheat oven to 325°. Remove plastic wrap and bake for 45 minutes. Check doneness by inserting the tip of a knife into the center of pudding. The knife should come out clean. If it doesn't, cook for 5 minutes more and test again.

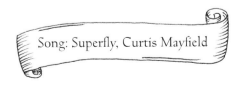

Song: Superfly, Curtis Mayfield

CRAB CAKES & EGGS
WITH CHIPOTLE AIOLI & CILANTRO PESTO

When the Red Aunts were touring the U.S., we found this amazing little crab shack in Baltimore that had the best crab cakes I had ever eaten. You walked into a blue shack, literally a shack—no tables, no chairs—and ordered at a little counter. The crab cakes were huge and came steaming hot, simply wrapped in brown butcher paper.

Those crab cakes were the inspiration for this wonderful brunch recipe, which I like to serve on a bed of greens. You can also serve them as hors d'oeuvres. Make them the size of golf balls and reduce the frying time to about 1 minute per side, or until lightly golden brown.

For advice on where to buy crab, see Crabby Deviled Eggs, page 34. For advice on choosing eggs for poaching, see Garden Lettuce & Herbs with the Perfect Poached Egg, page 26.

One final note: Poaching eight eggs at once is not a task for a rank beginner. It's not hard once you get the hang of it, but before inviting a crowd for brunch, practice your poaching!

Makes 8 crab cakes (serves 4)

FOR CRAB CAKES:

2 tablespoons unsalted butter, plus 4 tablespoons for frying

2 tablespoons olive oil, plus 1/4 cup for frying

3/4 cup finely chopped red onion

1 1/2 cups finely chopped celery

1/2 cup finely chopped red bell pepper

1/2 cup finely chopped yellow bell pepper

1 tablespoon capers, drained and rinsed

1/2 teaspoon Sriracha chile paste

1/2 teaspoon Worcestershire sauce

1 1/2 teaspoons Old Bay seasoning

1 teaspoon sea salt

1/2 teaspoon freshly ground pepper

1/2 pound lump crab meat, cleaned and picked over

2 1/2 cups coarse breadcrumbs

1/4 cup flat-leaf parsley, minced

1/2 cup mayonnaise

2 teaspoons Dijon mustard

Juice of 1 lemon

2 large eggs, lightly beaten

Heat 2 tablespoons butter and 2 tablespoons olive oil in a large sauté pan over medium heat. Add red onion, celery, bell peppers, capers, Sriracha, Worcestershire, Old Bay, salt, and pepper. Cook, stirring occasionally, until vegetables are soft, about 20 minutes. Remove vegetable mixture from heat and let cool.

In a large bowl, gently break up any very large pieces of crab meat but leave the medium and smaller chunks whole. Fold in breadcrumbs, parsley, mayonnaise, mustard, lemon juice, and beaten eggs. Add cooled vegetable mixture and gently mix until just incorporated. Cover and refrigerate for 30 minutes.

Preheat oven to 250°. Divide crab mixture into eight portions and form each into a round about 3 inches in diameter. In a large sauté pan, heat remaining 4 tablespoons butter and 1/4 cup olive oil. When pan is hot, add 4 crab cakes and fry, flipping once, until golden brown, about 4 to 5 minutes per side. Drain on paper towels. Transfer paper towels with crab cakes to a baking sheet and place in oven to keep warm. Repeat with remaining crab cakes.

FOR POACHED EGGS:

8 very fresh eggs
1 teaspoon apple cider vinegar

8 teaspoons Cilantro Pesto (*see recipe page 192*)
8 teaspoons Chipotle Aioli (*see recipe page 193*)

Fill a wide, deep saucepan with about 4 inches water. Add vinegar and a pinch of salt and bring to a boil. Reduce heat so water remains at a gentle boil.

Prepare 4 plates for serving and place 2 crab cakes on each. (You can put them on a bed of spring greens if you like.) Set aside.

Break 1 egg at a time into a small ramekin and tip egg into the water. Immediately repeat with remaining 7 eggs. Poach about 1 1/2 minutes for runny yolks, a bit more if you like firmer eggs. Lift out first egg with a slotted spoon and gently press the outside edge to make sure it is cooked to your liking. If so, rest spoon on a paper towel for a few seconds to drain excess water and place egg atop a crab cake. Repeat with remaining eggs.

Drizzle each egg-topped crab cake with 1 teaspoon Cilantro Pesto and 1 teaspoon Chipotle Aioli. Serve immediately.

ARTICHOKE BAKED EGGS

Artichokes are one of my favorite vegetables. This recipe is particularly great for using up leftover steamed artichokes from dinner the night before.

Serves 6

1 lemon
3 large artichokes
1 teaspoon sea salt, more to taste
Freshly ground pepper
1/2 cup panko breadcrumbs
3/4 cup good parmesan, preferably
    Parmigiano Reggiano, divided

6 large eggs
6 tablespoons unsalted butter, melted
4 thyme sprigs
4 small rosemary sprigs

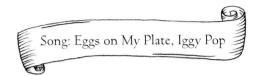

Song: Eggs on My Plate, Iggy Pop

Preheat oven to 350°.

Fill a medium mixing bowl with ice water. Squeeze juice of lemon into bowl. Trim stems off the bottom of each artichoke and cut each in half lengthwise. Immediately after slicing, submerge artichoke halves in lemon water to keep their color bright and prevent them from oxidizing. With a paring knife, remove the fuzzy choke from the center of each artichoke half.

Place trimmed artichokes in a medium stockpot filled three-quarters full with water. Add 1 teaspoon salt and bring to a boil. Reduce heat to medium-low, cover, and cook artichokes until they are tender when you insert a knife into the heart, about 35 minutes. Remove artichokes and set aside.

In a small bowl, combine breadcrumbs and 1/2 cup parmesan. Add a pinch of salt and a couple of grinds of fresh pepper.

Place artichokes, bottom side down, on a baking sheet. Crack 1 egg into center of each, taking care not to break the yolks. Sprinkle breadcrumb mixture atop each artichoke and drizzle with melted butter. Scatter rosemary and thyme sprigs on top and around artichokes. Bake until yolks are set but still runny, about 8 minutes. Sprinkle remaining 1/4 cup parmesan over the artichokes. Serve immediately.

CRABBY DEVILED EGGS

These delicious deviled eggs were inspired by a brunch I enjoyed while sitting outside at a lovely little restaurant in the Ferry Building in San Francisco. Pair them with a Bloody Mary for the perfect appetizer when your guests arrive. You can purchase crab from your fishmonger or at the fish counter in a quality grocery store. Specialty stores also have good canned crab claw meat. Pick over the meat to remove any leftover bits of shell.

Makes 48 deviled eggs

24 large eggs
1/4 cup white wine vinegar
1 cup mayonnaise
3/4 cup sour cream
1 tablespoon Dijon mustard
1 tablespoon Creole seasoning
1/2 teaspoon cayenne pepper
Juice and zest of 2 lemons

1/2 teaspoon sea salt, more to taste
1/4 teaspoon freshly ground pepper,
    more to taste
1 pound lump crab meat, cleaned and
    picked over, 1/4 cup reserved for garnish
3/4 cup chopped chives, white and tender
    green stems only, divided

For eggs:

Place eggs in a large saucepan and add cold water until they are covered by 1 inch. Add vinegar and bring water to a boil over medium-high heat. When water reaches a boil, cover the pan, turn off the heat, and leave on the stove for 12 minutes. Transfer eggs to a colander and run cold water over them to stop the cooking process. Peel and cut eggs in half lengthwise. Remove yolks and set aside.

For filling:

In a food processor, combine egg yolks, mayonnaise, sour cream, mustard, Creole seasoning, cayenne pepper, lemon juice and zest, salt, and pepper and purée until smooth. Add all but 1/4 cup crab and pulse two or three times, just until no large lumps remain. Remove from processor, fold in all but 2 tablespoons chives, and season with salt and pepper to taste.

Spoon filling into egg whites or pipe them through a pastry bag for a polished finish. Garnish with reserved crab and chives. Cover and chill in refrigerator for at least 1 hour before serving.

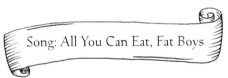

Song: All You Can Eat, Fat Boys

Hard Boiling Eggs

It is nearly impossible to peel "fresh" hard-boiled eggs. What I mean by fresh eggs is ones that are only a day or two old, which is typical of eggs from farmers' markets. Eggs from the supermarket are generally weeks old.

If your eggs are truly fresh, keep them in the fridge for a week before hard boiling them. And don't forget to add a teaspoon of salt to the water—it helps the proteins firm up, which makes the whites easier to separate from the shell, which will make them easier to peel. Eggs that are older than six or seven days are also easier to peel because their higher pH content strengthens their membranes. You can simulate this effect by adding a half teaspoon of baking soda per quart of cooking water, to make the water more alkaline.

VEGETARIAN RED FLANNEL HASH

I love this beautiful and tasty spring dish because everything is made in a cast iron skillet in the oven. Traditionally, hash is made with corned beef, but this version is vegetarian. Dice all the vegetables uniformly so they cook evenly, and use the freshest eggs you can find.

Serves 4

1/4 cup plus 2 tablespoons vegetable oil, divided
5 medium red potatoes, finely chopped
5 small beets, peeled and finely chopped
1 small yellow onion, finely chopped
3 cloves garlic, minced
Sea salt and freshly ground pepper
1/4 cup finely chopped flat-leaf parsley
2 tablespoons finely chopped dill
4 large eggs

Preheat oven to 450° and arrange rack in middle of oven.

Pour 1/4 cup oil into a large cast iron skillet. Place skillet in oven until hot and oil is sizzling, about 5 minutes.

Meanwhile, in a large bowl, toss remaining 2 tablespoons oil with potatoes, beets, onion, and garlic. Sprinkle generously with salt and pepper and mix well. Distribute vegetable mixture evenly in hot skillet and roast until vegetables caramelize and are slightly crisp, about 25 minutes.

Remove skillet from oven and stir vegetables well, scraping any brown bits from the bottom of the pan. Sprinkle with parsley and dill. Make 4 shallow, 3-inch indentations in the vegetables and crack an egg into each. Return skillet to oven and roast until eggs reach desired doneness, about 3 minutes for slightly runny eggs. Season with salt and pepper to taste. Serve immediately.

Song: Flavor, Jon Spencer Blues Explosion

Song: Feelin' Good, Jessie Mae Hemphill

SCALLOPED NEW POTATOES WITH AGED CHEDDAR

I like using new potatoes in this recipe because you don't have to peel them. They're harvested early, so they have very thin skins and are high in moisture content, which makes them really nice for cooking. You can find new potatoes in the spring at your local farmers' market or at quality supermarkets. You can substitute three brown-skinned baking potatoes if you can't get your hands on new potatoes, but you will need to peel them.

Serves 4

2 tablespoons unsalted butter
1/4 cup finely chopped onion
1/2 teaspoon freshly grated nutmeg
1/2 teaspoon cayenne pepper
2 tablespoons flour
1 1/4 cups whole milk

1 cup good cheddar cheese (such as Hook's or Cabot Clothbound), divided
Sea salt and freshly ground pepper
15 new potatoes, not rinsed but any bad spots removed, thinly sliced
Nonstick cooking spray

Preheat oven to 350°.

Melt butter in a medium saucepan over medium heat. Add onions and cook until soft, about 5 minutes. Add nutmeg and cayenne. Whisk in flour and cook for about 3 minutes, lowering the heat a bit if it starts bubbling rapidly (you want a slow bubble, not a fast one). Add milk, whisking constantly until roux thickens, about 1 to 2 minutes. Remove from heat and stir in 3/4 cup cheddar. Season with salt and pepper to taste.

Spray a 9″ × 9″ glass or stoneware baking dish with nonstick spray. Layer half the potato slices in the pan, sprinkle lightly with salt and pepper, and ladle half the sauce on top of potatoes. Repeat, finishing with sauce. Sprinkle with remaining 1/4 cup cheese.

Spray a piece of foil with nonstick spray and loosely cover potatoes with foil, greased side down (to prevent cheese from sticking). Bake until potatoes are tender, about 30 minutes. Remove foil and continue baking until top is lightly browned, about 5 minutes. Serve immediately.

ASPARAGUS WITH GREMOLATA

When buying asparagus, look for medium to thick spears—counter intuitively, they're tenderer than thin spears. Also make sure that the tips don't look dried out. If you're not going to use them right away, wrap a wet paper towel around the bottom of the spears to keep them fresh and hydrated.

This dish can be served hot or at room temperature. I like to add the chilled spears to sandwiches or chop them up in salads.

VARIATION: Instead of roasting the asparagus, try grilling it.

Serves 6

2 tablespoons extra-virgin olive oil
2 bunches thick fresh asparagus
1 teaspoon sea salt

1 teaspoon freshly ground pepper
1 teaspoon herbes de Provence

GREMOLATA:

3 tablespoons finely chopped flat-leaf parsley
1 teaspoon lemon zest
2 garlic cloves, finely minced

Song: Little Friend, The Ponys

Preheat oven to 450°.

Line a rimmed baking sheet with foil and drizzle with olive oil. Trim the tough root ends off the asparagus and spread out spears evenly on baking sheet. Sprinkle with salt, pepper, and herbes de Provence. Shake the pan gently to roll the asparagus around and coat them with the seasonings. Roast until spears turn bright green, about 6 minutes. Be careful not to overcook or they will turn yellowish green.

While asparagus roasts, prepare the Gremolata. In a small bowl, mix together parsley, lemon zest, and garlic. Set aside.

Transfer asparagus to a serving platter. Sprinkle with gremolata and season with salt and pepper to taste. Serve immediately.

RHUBARB COMPOTE

Rhubarb, which looks like reddish-green celery stalks when raw, is very tart. Cook it up with some sugar, and it turns into a deliciously sweet and tangy concoction. While rhubarb is mostly used in dessert recipes, this compote works beautifully on pancakes, french toast, regular toast, granola, yogurt, or anything else you'd top with jam. You can serve it hot or cold.

Makes about 2 cups

3 cups chopped rhubarb (about 1 large bunch, root ends trimmed)
1/2 cup sugar
1 teaspoon lemon juice

Combine the rhubarb, sugar, and lemon juice in a medium saucepan over medium heat. Cook, stirring every 2 to 3 minutes, until mixture thickens and has the consistency of oatmeal, about 20 to 25 minutes. Remove from heat. The compote will thicken as it cools. Refrigerate for up to a week.

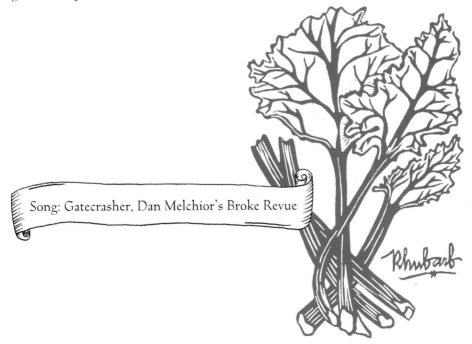

Song: Gatecrasher, Dan Melchior's Broke Revue

INDIAN SPICED ROASTED CARROTS

I am so in love with the beautiful carrots I find at my local farmers' markets. They taste worlds apart from the ones at the supermarket. They're sweeter and have a richer flavor. If you're lucky, you can get them in many different colors—red, purple, white, yellow, and an almost blackish purple that is orange inside—but they all taste pretty much the same.

I like the beautiful knobby skin, so I don't peel my carrots. I just scrub them with a coarse sponge. Before roasting, make sure they are completely dry so they crisp up nicely. These carrots are lovely as a side dish or sliced, tossed with some greens, and served as a salad.

Serves 4

2 bunches small to medium carrots,
   tops trimmed
1 tablespoon ground cumin
1 tablespoon ground coriander
1 teaspoon cayenne pepper

1/2 cup shelled, unsalted pistachios
1/2 cup extra-virgin olive oil
1 teaspoon sea salt
3 twists freshly ground pepper

Preheat oven to 375°.

Scrub carrots and cut in half lengthwise so you can see the beautiful colors inside. Towel dry and set aside.

Place a small frying pan over medium heat and add cumin, coriander, cayenne, and pistachios. Toast, stirring occasionally, until spices smell fragrant, about 2 minutes. Remove from heat to cool slightly. Pulse the mixture in a mini food processor until the nuts are roughly chopped. Alternatively, use a spice grinder, but be careful not to chop the nuts too finely.

Place carrots and olive oil in a large bowl and mix well. Add salt, pepper, and spice mixture. Toss again until the carrots are well coated.

Line a rimmed baking sheet with foil and spread out carrots evenly. Bake until carrots begin to caramelize and the tips turn brown, about 15 minutes. Season with salt and pepper to taste. Serve immediately.

Song: Imaginary Person, Ty Segall

SUMMER

SUMMER RECIPES

Peach, Burrata, Prosciutto & Hazelnut Salad

Spicy Melon & Peanut Salad

Orzo, Tomato, Arugula & Kalamata Olive Salad

Heirloom Bean & Tomato Salad

Best Cobb Ever

Granola & Yogurt Parfait

Mabel's Short Stack

Orange Ciabatta French Toast with Berries

Tomato, Avocado & Fried Egg Tartine

Tomato & Goat Cheese Frittata

Tomato & Spinach Frittata with
Green Tomato Chow Chow

Zucchini & Potato Hash Browns with
Poached Eggs & Sweet 100 Tomatoes

Baked Eggs in Spicy Tomato Sauce

Tomato & Onion Provençal

WHAT'S IN SEASON IN SUMMER?

Basil
Beets
Blackberries
Blueberries
Cantaloupe
Carrots
Chiles
Cilantro
Cucumber
Eggplant
Fennel
Figs
Grapes
Green Beans

Green Onions
Melon
Peaches
Peppers
Plums
Pluots
Radishes
Raspberries
Shelling beans
Strawberries
Summer squash
Tomatillos
Tomatoes
Watermelon

The Only Good Thing About Summer

Hot, hot summer! I'm a cold-weather person, so I always say that the only good thing about summer is the produce. My garden goes crazy in the California heat, and the farmers' markets overflow with the most beautiful things: heirloom tomatoes, loads of different summer squash, melons as sweet as candy, eggplants from white to the darkest purple, stone fruit that's at the height of flavor. It's almost worth the heat—but I still try my best to stay cool, which is why so many of my summer recipes do not involve turning on the oven.

At Auntie Em's, all of our cobblers, crisps, and pies use the fruit that's in season. So from late fall through early spring, we joke that all we have are pears and apples. As soon as the farm calls and says the first of the apricots are ripe, we celebrate, because for the next few months we'll have cherries, peaches, plums, nectarines, grapes, and pluots.

My favorite of all the summer bounties is the tomato. I've been carrying on a love affair with the tomato my whole life. I grew them in pots on the tiny front porch at my very first apartment in downtown Fullerton. I've planted tomatoes every summer since, no matter where I lived, and nowadays, in my Eagle Rock backyard, I have six large beds, where I grow everything from tiny Sweet Pea Currant tomatoes to Yellow Jumbos and Mortgage Lifters. At the end of the summer, I make loads of tomato sauce and also freeze blanched, skinned tomatoes to use later in soups, stews, and sauces. I also can salsas, chow chows, and chutneys, which are so easy to pop out year-round to top frittatas, quiches, scrambled eggs, and baked egg dishes. We serve salsa with all of our egg dishes at Auntie Em's.

I may not like the heat, but I still love to host get-togethers in my garden in summertime. I invite people for Sunday mornings, before it gets too hot, and serve brunch. Here's the typical scene: lots of vintage tablecloths layered on the table, unmatched linen napkins, peach and nectarine bellinis, a beautiful stone-fruit crostada, scones, French butter (I call it "ten-dollar butter"), a bowl of berries, a platter of thick-cut bacon, and a nice tomato and goat cheese frittata. Never mind the heat—it's heaven!

Peach, Burrata, Prosciutto & Hazelnut Salad

This salad is a great alternative to a caprese. Peaches instead of the more common tomatoes sweeten things up a bit. The dressing makes more than you'll need, so save it for your next salad—it's a great all-around vinaigrette.

Serves 4

For the vinaigrette:
2 teaspoons minced shallot
1 teaspoon Dijon mustard
1/3 cup Champagne vinegar
1 cup extra-virgin olive oil
1 teaspoon sea salt, plus more to taste
1/2 teaspoon freshly ground pepper,
    plus more to taste

Combine shallots, mustard, vinegar, olive oil, salt, and pepper in a medium jar with a lid. Seal lid and vigorously shake until vinaigrette is emulsified.

For the salad:
6 cups wild baby arugula
1/3 cup Champagne vinaigrette, recipe above
1 large ball (1 pound) burrata cheese, sliced into 4 wedges
8 slices prosciutto, thinly sliced crosswise
2 very ripe peaches, cored and each sliced into 8 wedges
1 cup hazelnuts, toasted and roughly chopped

In a medium bowl, toss arugula with dressing. Divide arugula on 4 chilled salad bowls or plates and nestle a slice of burrata alongside each. Top each salad with 1/4 of prosciutto, peaches, and hazelnuts. Season with salt and pepper to taste. Serve immediately.

SPICY MELON & PEANUT SALAD

If you have not had a melon fresh from the garden or from the farmers' market, you have not had a melon. The burst of flavor in your mouth screams summer. Donna, the head chef at Auntie Em's, created this recipe for our chilled salad case. She prefers using striped Charentais melons, also known as French cantaloupe, because of their flavor complexity. If you can't find a Charentais, you can use any heirloom variety, such as Casaba, Crenshaw, Canary, Piel De Sapo, Sherlyn, or White Crenshaw. You can find heirloom melons at many farmers' markets or such specialty stores as Whole Foods and Trader Joe's.

Serves 4 as a side salad

4 cups French cantaloupe (Charentais), peeled and cut into 1-inch dice
1 Persian cucumber, peeled and cut into 1-inch dice
1 jalapeño pepper, seeded and minced, or to taste
1-inch piece ginger, peeled and minced
1/4 cup mint chiffonade
1/4 cup cilantro chiffonade
Juice of 2 limes, or more to taste
1/2 cup unsalted peanuts, toasted and chopped roughly
Sea salt and freshly ground pepper

Lightly toss together all ingredients in a large bowl. Season with salt, pepper, and additional lime juice to taste. Serve immediately.

Song: Hot Pants, James Brown

ORZO, TOMATO, ARUGULA & KALAMATA OLIVE SALAD

This salad has been a daily staple since Auntie Em's opened. It holds up really well, making it the perfect side to bring to a friend's house or a picnic. Wild arugula is a cultivated variety that you can find at farmers' markets and better supermarkets. It is spicier than regular arugula.

Serves 4 as a side dish

1 teaspoon sea salt, plus more to taste
1 cup orzo pasta
1/4 cup extra-virgin olive oil
1 clove garlic, minced
2 tablespoons Champagne vinegar
2 tablespoons fresh lemon juice
Sea salt and freshly ground pepper

Song: Little Olive, The Electric Prunes

1 cup teardrop, sweet 100s, or any other small tomato, cut in half
2 cups wild baby arugula (or regular baby arugula)
1/2 cup kalamata olives, roughly chopped
1/2 cup feta cheese, crumbled
1/4 cup pine nuts, toasted

Fill a medium saucepan halfway with water, add salt, and bring to a boil. Stir in orzo. Boil, stirring occasionally, until al dente, about 9 minutes or according to package instructions. Drain and set aside to cool.

While the orzo cools, make the vinaigrette. In a small bowl, whisk together olive oil, garlic, vinegar, and lemon juice. Season with salt and pepper to taste.

To assemble the salad, combine tomatoes, arugula, olives, feta, pine nuts, and orzo in a large bowl. Add 2/3 of vinaigrette and gently toss. Season with salt and pepper, and add additional vinaigrette to taste. Serve at room temperature or chilled.

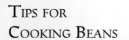

TIPS FOR
COOKING BEANS

- Pre-soak beans for at least
  4 hours.
- Add such aromatics as
  garlic, onions, or bay leaves
  to the water while cooking.
- Let beans cool in the
  cooking water with the
  aromatics so they soak up
  the flavorful liquid.

Song: Here Comes the Summer, The Undertones

HEIRLOOM BEAN & TOMATO SALAD

This recipe is much better if you cook your own beans from scratch. I love to use dried heirloom beans, like those from Rancho Gordo, which you can buy online. Keep in mind that fresh beans like theirs will cook much faster than many supermarket beans.

Serves 6 as a side salad

1 cup dried heirloom beans, such as cannellini, flageolet, or cranberry, soaked in water for at least 4 hours and drained

4 sprigs thyme

4 small sprigs rosemary

3 cloves garlic, peeled and smashed

1 small yellow onion, quartered

1 stalk celery, roughly chopped

1 1/2 teaspoons sea salt, plus more to taste

1 large shallot, finely chopped

3 oil-packed anchovy fillets, drained and finely chopped

3 tablespoons red wine vinegar

1/2 cup extra-virgin olive oil

1/4 teaspoon freshly ground pepper, plus more to taste

1 pound multi-colored heirloom cherry tomatoes, cut in half, or large heirloom tomatoes chopped into 1/2-inch dice

1/2 cup roughly chopped basil

2 sprigs oregano, leaves only, roughly chopped

Place beans in a deep, heavy-bottomed pot and cover with 6 to 8 cups cold water, enough to cover the beans by 2 inches. Add thyme, rosemary, garlic, onion, celery, and 1 teaspoon salt. Bring to a boil over high heat, then reduce heat to a gentle simmer. Cover and cook until beans are tender, about 1 hour, occasionally skimming any foam that rises to the surface. Cooking time varies depending on the freshness of your beans. Remove from heat and allow beans to cool completely in broth.

In a large bowl, combine shallots, anchovies, vinegar, 1/2 teaspoon salt, and pepper. Slowly whisk in olive oil until vinaigrette is emulsified. Drain cooled beans and add them to the bowl. Add tomatoes and lightly toss vegetables with the dressing. Let stand at room temperature for at least 2 hours.

Fold in basil and oregano and season with salt and pepper to taste. Serve at room temperature.

BEST COBB EVER

I know I'm biased, but I really do think this is the best Cobb salad I have ever had. I put a lot of thought into how I wanted it to taste: the crunch, the mouth feel, the flavor combination in each bite. Yes, I'm obsessive! The secret to this salad is making sure everything is at its freshest and the tomatoes are from your garden or the farmers' market—and are ripe. Instead of a creamy dressing, I use a vinaigrette, because the salad gets enough creaminess from the egg and blue cheese. Butter lettuce is also a must. It's so crunchy and juicy, and it holds up to the dressing.

Serves 4

8 cups roughly chopped butter lettuce
3 cups chopped teardrop, sweet 100s, or any other small tomato
4 hard-boiled eggs, finely chopped
2 cups finely chopped scallions, including any tender green stems
10 slices applewood-smoked bacon, cooked until crispy and roughly chopped
1 1/2 cups good blue cheese (such as Point Reyes Blue or Jasper Hills Farm Blue)
2 cooked skinless, boneless chicken breast halves, chilled and roughly chopped into
   1/2-inch cubes
1/2 cup Apple Cider Vinaigrette (*see recipe page 193*), plus more to taste
Sea salt and freshly ground pepper

Chill a large metal bowl in the freezer for 5 minutes.

Combine all ingredients in bowl and gently toss until dressing is evenly coated. Season with salt, pepper, and additional vinaigrette to taste. Divide salad between 4 chilled bowls or plates and top each with a grind or two of pepper.

Song: Summertime Blues, Blue Cheer

GRANOLA & YOGURT PARFAIT

We serve this parfait with yogurt, but it's also great with milk.

Makes 4 parfaits

FOR GRANOLA:
Nonstick cooking spray or unsalted butter, for baking sheet
3 cups old-fashioned oats
1 cup slivered almonds
1 1/3 cups sweetened, shredded coconut
6 tablespoons plus 1 1/2 teaspoons honey
1/2 cup plus 2 tablespoons vegetable oil
1/4 teaspoon almond extract
3/4 teaspoon vanilla extract

Preheat oven to 350°. Lightly coat a baking sheet with nonstick cooking spray or butter.

In a medium bowl, combine oats, almonds, and coconut. Set aside.

In a small bowl, whisk together honey, oil, and extracts. Pour honey mixture into dry ingredients, mix well, and distribute mixture evenly on baking sheet. Bake until all ingredients are a deep golden brown, stirring every 5 minutes to ensure even baking, about 20 minutes total. Watch carefully the last few minutes to avoid burning the granola. Cool completely on baking sheet.

ASSEMBLING THE PARFAIT:
4 cups homemade granola
2 cups good-quality plain yogurt (such as Strauss)
2 cups mixed in-season berries, such as raspberries, blueberries, and sliced strawberries

Place 1 cup granola and 1/2 cup yogurt in 4 parfait glasses or serving bowls. Top each with 1/2 cup berries. Serve immediately.

Song: Pleasure, Girls at Our Best!

MABEL'S SHORT STACK

This is one of the most popular dishes on our menu, and, not surprisingly, it was inspired by an Ina Garten recipe. Before I opened Auntie Em's, I went to a cookbook signing that she did at UCLA. We really hit it off, so we went out with some friends of mine for drinks after the signing. I ended up sharing an appetizer recipe with her that she used in one of her cookbooks. When I was getting ready to open Auntie Em's, I often talked with Ina on the phone, and she gave me lots of good pointers and tips on running a café. She was really a big help.

As for the name of the dish, it's in honor of my friend Jimmy Hole's dog, Mabel, who has very short legs.

There are three important keys to this recipe. Whipping the egg whites makes the pancakes light and fluffy. Make sure to whip them until stiff peaks form. Topping the cakes with the freshest in-season fruit is also key. Berries and stone fruit work best, but get creative according to what's in season and what you find at the farmers' market. And lastly, use only pure maple syrup!

Makes 12 4-inch pancakes

1 1/2 cups flour
2 tablespoons plus 2 teaspoons granulated sugar
1 tablespoon plus 1 teaspoon brown sugar
2 teaspoons baking powder
3/4 teaspoon baking soda
1/4 teaspoon sea salt
2 large eggs, separated
1 1/3 cups buttermilk
4 tablespoons (2 ounces) butter, melted,
   plus more for cooking pancakes
1 teaspoon vanilla extract
4 cups mixed in-season fruit, such as blackberries, raspberries, blueberries,
   sliced strawberries, peaches, pluots, plums, and/or figs
Pure maple syrup, warmed, for serving

Preheat oven to 200°. In a large bowl, mix flour, sugars, baking powder, baking soda, and salt. Set aside.

In a small bowl, mix egg yolks, buttermilk, butter, and vanilla extract. Add to dry ingredients and mix well.

Using a stand mixer, hand mixer, or whisk, whip egg whites until stiff peaks form (the peaks should hold their shape). Gently fold egg whites into batter until just combined, no more.

Heat a medium sauté pan, cast iron skillet, or griddle over medium-high heat. When the pan is hot, add enough butter to lightly coat the bottom of the pan and pour in 1/4 cup batter. Cook until pancake is golden brown on the bottom, about 1 to 2 minutes after bubbles begin to form in the center. Flip and cook until golden brown on the other side, about 1 to 2 minutes longer. Total cooking time is about 5 to 6 minutes. Remove pancake to a plate and repeat with remaining batter, adding more butter as needed.

To serve, place 4 plates in the oven until warm, about 5 minutes. Divide pancakes between plates and top each with 1 cup of fruit. Serve immediately with maple syrup.

Song: California Paradise, The Runaways

ORANGE CIABATTA FRENCH TOAST WITH BERRIES

Auntie Em's french toast is very popular, but it's not for the faint of heart. It's rich, crunchy, and amazingly delicious. When you're ready for a treat, go for it!

Serves 4

Zest of 1 medium orange
1/3 cup fresh orange juice
1/4 cup milk
1/4 cup heavy cream
1/2 teaspoon vanilla extract
1 teaspoon honey
2 large eggs
8 slices ciabatta bread, sliced 1 inch thick
1/4 cup vegetable oil
1 tablespoon unsalted butter
4 cups mixed in-season berries, such as blueberries, blackberries, and sliced strawberries
Powdered sugar for garnish, optional

In a large, shallow baking dish, whisk together orange zest and juice, milk, cream, vanilla, honey, and eggs until well combined.

Partially submerge each bread slice in egg mixture for 15 minutes. Flip over each slice and repeat.

Heat vegetable oil and butter in a large, nonstick skillet over medium-high heat. Cook 4 pieces of bread at a time until golden brown, flipping once, about 2 minutes per side. Repeat with remaining bread.

Divide french toast between 4 plates and top each with 1 cup berries. Dust with powdered sugar if you like. Serve immediately.

TOMATO, AVOCADO & FRIED EGG TARTINE

A large part of our breakfast menu centers on tartines, which are simply open-faced sandwiches. You can really riff on this sandwich with your favorite ingredients: bacon, tomato and egg, roasted vegetables and eggs, meatloaf and eggs, brie and roasted mushrooms with eggs, ham and aged cheddar and eggs, you name it.

Serves 4

4 slices good-quality whole wheat bread, toasted
4 slices Gruyère cheese
1 large heirloom tomato, cut into 4 1/2-inch slices
1 large avocado
2 teaspoons extra-virgin olive oil
4 large eggs
Sea salt and freshly ground pepper

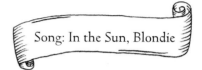
Song: In the Sun, Blondie

Preheat broiler to high.

Top each piece of toast with a slice of cheese. Broil until cheese is melted and just beginning to brown, about 1 to 3 minutes, depending on your broiler. Divide cheese toasts among 4 plates and top each with a tomato slice.

Slice avocado in half lengthwise and remove pit. Place avocado in your hand, skin side down, and slice flesh in thin strips with a pairing knife. Take care not to pierce the skin. Repeat with second half. Set aside.

Heat olive oil in a large skillet over medium-high heat. When skillet is hot, crack eggs one by one and gently slide each into the skillet. Fry eggs, flipping once, until the edges are beginning to turn golden brown and the center is set but still runny, approximately 2 minutes per side. Place an egg on top of each tartine.

With a large spoon, scoop out the avocado slices. Fan a quarter of the slices slightly alongside each egg, taking care not to break the yolk. Season with salt and pepper to taste. Serve immediately.

The Auntie Em's Cookbook

TOMATO & GOAT CHEESE FRITTATA

Firm tomatoes that hold their shape work best in this recipe. The frittata is lovely served with a small, simple salad.

Serves 6 for a main course, more as a side dish

12 large eggs
1/4 cup heavy cream
1/4 cup whole milk
2 teaspoons ground nutmeg
2 teaspoons cayenne pepper
2 teaspoons sea salt, plus more to taste
2 teaspoons freshly ground pepper, plus more to taste
2 tablespoons extra-virgin olive oil
1 small log (4 to 4.5 ounces) goat cheese, crumbled
1 medium tomato, thinly sliced
1 small zucchini, finely diced
2 jalapeños, seeded and minced
3 tablespoons basil chiffonade, divided

Song: Sunny Afternoon, The Kinks

Preheat oven to 350°.

In a large bowl, whisk together eggs, cream, milk, nutmeg, cayenne, salt, and pepper.

Heat olive oil in a 12-inch cast iron or heavy-bottomed skillet over medium-high heat. When skillet is hot, add egg mixture. Evenly distribute goat cheese, tomato slices, zucchini, jalapeños, and 1 1/2 tablespoons basil throughout eggs. Reduce heat to medium and cook until bottom of frittata begins to brown, about 5 minutes. Check this by lifting an edge of the eggs with a spatula.

Place frittata in oven and bake until center is just set (no longer than that), about 8 minutes. Slide frittata onto a heat-proof cutting board and slice into wedges. Top each slice with remaining 1 1/2 tablespoons basil. Season with salt and pepper to taste. Serve hot or at room temperature.

Song: Sunshine Girl, The Dirtbombs

Tomato & Spinach Frittata with Green Tomato Chow Chow

Chow chow gives this frittata a tangy zip that can be a bit intense at breakfast, so I like to serve it for lunch. For a colorful top to your frittata, use different colors of heirloom tomatoes.

Serves 6 as a main course, more as a side dish

12 large eggs
1/4 cup whole milk
1/4 cup heavy cream
2 teaspoons ground nutmeg
2 teaspoons cayenne pepper
2 teaspoon sea salt, plus more to taste
2 teaspoon freshly ground pepper, plus more to taste
2 tablespoons extra-virgin olive oil
4 1/2 ounces good parmesan, preferably Parmigiano Reggiano, grated
2 medium heirloom tomatoes, thinly sliced
2 cups fresh spinach, stemmed and roughly chopped
3/4 cup Green Tomato & Zucchini Chow Chow (*see recipe page 86*)

Preheat oven to 350°.

In a large bowl, whisk together eggs, milk, cream, nutmeg, cayenne, salt, and pepper. Heat olive oil in a 12-inch cast iron or heavy-bottomed skillet over medium-high heat. When skillet is hot, add egg mixture. Evenly distribute parmesan, tomato slices, and spinach throughout eggs. Reduce heat to medium and cook until bottom of frittata begins to brown, about 5 minutes. Check this by lifting an edge of the eggs with a spatula.

Place frittata in oven and bake until center is just set (no longer), about 8 minutes. Slide frittata onto a heat-proof cutting board and slice into wedges. Top each slice with about 2 tablespoons chow chow, Season to taste with salt and pepper. Serve hot or at room temperature.

ZUCCHINI & POTATO HASH BROWNS
WITH POACHED EGGS & SWEET 100 TOMATOES

We all need to eat more veggies, so why not start with breakfast? The hash browns are crunchy and a bit salty, and the Sweet 100 cherry tomatoes give the dish a balance of tangy and sweet. If you can't find Sweet 100s, use the best cherry tomatoes you can find.

Make sure you use a large, nonstick sauté pan. The size of the pan and the nonstick surface make flipping the hash browns and sliding them out of the pan easy. And don't be afraid to try flipping the potatoes in the air. It's fun!

Serves 4

6 medium fingerling potatoes
1 large zucchini
2 sprigs thyme, leaves only
1 teaspoon sea salt, plus more to taste
1/4 teaspoon freshly ground pepper, plus more to taste
2 tablespoons vegetable oil
1 teaspoon apple cider vinegar
4 very fresh large eggs
1/2 cup halved Sweet 100 or other cherry tomatoes
Small handful finely chopped chives

Song: Hang a Picture, Thee Oh Sees

The Auntie Em's Cookbook

Preheat oven to 350°.

Grate potatoes on the largest holes of a box grater. Rinse grated potato in a colander and squeeze out water with your hands. Place potatoes on clean dish towel, roll up towel, and squeeze firmly to remove remaining water. Grate zucchini on same box grater. Do not rinse. Roll zucchini in a clean dish towel and squeeze to remove excess water as you did with potatoes.

In a medium bowl, mix together grated potatoes, zucchini, thyme, salt, and pepper.

Heat oil in a 12-inch nonstick sauté pan over high heat. When skillet is hot, distribute potato mixture evenly throughout pan. Use a large spatula or wood spoon to gently press down on potato mixture to compress it slightly in the pan. Reduce heat to medium-high and cook until potatoes are golden brown on the bottom, about 12 minutes. Use the spatula to press down on potatoes once more. Shake the pan to loosen the potatoes and quickly flip them over in one piece. If you prefer not to flip the potatoes in the air, cut them in half and flip each half with a spatula. Continue to cook until other side is golden brown, about another 12 minutes.

Place potatoes in oven and bake until crispy on the outside but still moist inside, about 25 minutes. Gently slide hash browns onto a large heat-proof cutting board. Slice in quarters, like a pie, and divide hash browns between 4 plates.

Meanwhile, fill a medium saucepan halfway full of water. Add vinegar and a pinch of salt and bring to a boil. Reduce heat so water remains at a gentle boil. Break 1 egg at a time into a small ramekin and tip egg into the water. Immediately repeat with remaining 3 eggs. Poach about 1 1/2 minutes for runny yolks, a bit more if you like firmer eggs. Lift out first egg with a slotted spoon and gently press the outside edge to make sure it is cooked to your liking. If so, rest spoon on a paper towel for a few seconds to drain excess water and place egg atop one serving of hashbrowns. Repeat with remaining eggs.

Sprinkle hash browns with tomatoes and chives. Season with salt and pepper to taste. Serve immediately.

BAKED EGGS IN SPICY TOMATO SAUCE

If I have unexpected company (it happens!), this is my quick, easy go-to dish. It is also a perfect way to use your jarred tomato sauce from the summer, and it's especially great when served with little garlic toasts to dip into the eggs and tomato sauce.

Serves 4

Song: Mater Dolores, The Screamers

2 tablespoons extra-virgin olive oil

1 shallot, minced

3 garlic cloves, minced

3 jalapeños, seeded and finely chopped

4 medium ripe and meaty tomatoes, chopped into 1-inch dice

1 teaspoon fresh rosemary, chopped

1 teaspoon fresh oregano leaves, chopped

2 teaspoons sea salt, plus more to taste

1/2 teaspoon freshly ground pepper, plus more to taste

4 eggs

1/4 cup grated good parmesan, preferably Parmigiano Reggiano

1/4 cup basil chiffonade

Preheat oven to 400°.

Heat olive oil in a medium saucepan over medium heat. Add shallots, garlic, and jalapeño and cook until shallots are translucent, about 1 minute. Add tomatoes, rosemary, oregano, salt, and pepper. Cook over low heat until the sauce begins to thicken, about 12 minutes. Taste and add salt and pepper to taste if desired. Set aside to cool for 10 minutes.

Purée sauce with a hand immersion blender or in a regular blender until smooth. Divide sauce between 4 ovenproof ramekins and crack an egg into each. Sprinkle parmesan on top of eggs. Place ramekins in oven and bake until egg whites are cooked but yolks are still runny, 8 to 10 minutes.

Sprinkle eggs with basil and season with salt and pepper to taste. Serve immediately.

Song: Dancing Days, Led Zeppelin

TOMATO & ONION PROVENÇAL

This lovely, layered dish is a great accompaniment for a fish, chicken, or beef main course.

Serves 4

Unsalted butter, for baking dish
1 cup coarse breadcrumbs
1/2 cup grated Pecorino Romano
1 tablespoon lemon zest
1 tablespoon thyme leaves
1 clove minced garlic
3 tablespoons extra-virgin olive oil
3 teaspoons sea salt, divided
1 1/2 teaspoons freshly ground pepper, divided
4 large, firm heirloom tomatoes, sliced into 1/2-inch rounds
1 red onion, cut into 1/4-inch slices

Preheat oven to 400° and lightly butter a 2-quart baking dish.

In a small bowl, combine breadcrumbs, pecorino romano, lemon zest, thyme, garlic, and olive oil. Mix well and season with 2 teaspoons salt and 1 teaspoon pepper.

Arrange tomato and onion slices in single alternating layers in baking dish, finishing with onions. Season with remaining 1 teaspoon salt and 1/2 teaspoon pepper. Sprinkle with breadcrumb mixture. Bake until onions are soft, about 20 to 25 minutes. Serve hot or at room temperature.

PRESERVING THE END OF SUMMER

Bread & Butter Pickles

Refrigerator Pickles

Spicy Pickled Beets

Dilly Beans

Quick Heirloom Tomato Sauce

Oven-dried Tomatoes in Olive Oil

Spicy Ketchup

Green Tomato & Zucchini Chow Chow

Laura Ann's Blueberry Basil Jam

Basil Pesto

Preserving the End of Summer & Listening to the Blues

The end of summer is a really exciting season in the kitchen. As my friend and head chef Donna says, "It's that magical time of the year when summer and fall vegetables come together." So preserve them! Then, in the dead of winter (we don't really have a dead of winter in L.A., but I like to pretend), you can pull out jars of summer tomatoes for your pastas and soups, early fall pickled beets for a winter citrus and beet salad, and crunchy pickles to serve with sandwiches or chop into slaws.

My friend Laura Ann started her own artisan jam business called Laura Ann's Jams. She plays around with wonderful combinations like blackberry bay leaf, strawberry vanilla bean, raspberry habañero, and the blueberry basil recipe she shared with me for this chapter. It's fun to play with flavor when you're pickling and preserving. There are no hard and fast rules to the flavor profiles, so go ahead and experiment.

We make our own compotes, ketchup, barbecue sauce, refrigerator pickles, and salsas at Auntie Em's. We go through all of it so fast that we don't need to preserve any. If this is the case with you, then all you need to do is keep whatever you make in sterilized jars in your fridge.

But if you want to preserve them for later use, it's not difficult. Canning has become popular again lately, so you may already know how. After you've made the pickles or jams, you can use what is called the boiling-water canning method to preserve your stash. When you preserve something using this method, you don't have to refrigerate it. You can store it in a cool, dry place for up to a year. In the pages that follow, I'll explain how.

I find myself listening to the blues when I'm canning. There's something so old school and therapeutic about listening to slide guitar and harmonica while stirring a compote—especially on a lazy afternoon at the hot end of summer.

Sterilizing Jars

You need to use mason jars, which are glass canning jars, to safely preserve. You can buy them at grocery and hardware stores or online, but be sure they are canning jars. Some glass jars, even those labeled as "mason" jars, are not meant for canning and cannot withstand extreme temperature changes. The top of the jar must be free of chips to seal properly. You need two-piece metal lids (a flat, center piece and ridged rim), not the single metal lids that you find on non-food jars.

I sterilize my jars even if I'm not going to use a hot water bath to preserve them, just to be safe. It is very important to use clean, sterilized jars so there is little chance for any bacteria growth.

1. Place jars and lids in a large stockpot of boiling water. Boil for 10 minutes, making sure they are completely submerged at all times. Carefully remove jars and lids from water with a jar lifter. Place upside down on paper towels or a clean kitchen towel to drain.
2. Using a funnel or ladle, fill jars with prepared food, leaving 1/4-inch headspace at top of each jar. Wipe inside rims clean with a paper towel soaked in hot water. Eliminate any air bubbles by poking a clean, non-metallic kitchen utensil like a wood skewer or rubber spatula into jar contents two or three times.
3. Close lids firmly with your hands. Lids should be secure but not totally air tight. Water should not be able to get in, but air needs to escape during the canning process.

How to Preserve

The boiling-water canning method is the simplest way to can. You want to have the right equipment, so I suggest buying or borrowing a boiling-water canner with a fitted lid and removable rack. A jar lifter is also helpful. You can purchase them online or at cooking stores. I like to use pint or quart jars, depending on the produce, but you can use any size. Just be sure to adjust the amount of water so the jars are completely covered by at least one to two inches of water at all times. For successful canning, follow the steps below.

1. Place wire rack in bottom of canning pot. Place canner on stove and fill halfway with warm water. Using a jar lifter, place as many sealed jars as recommended for your canner on rack. Make sure jar lifter is securely positioned below neck of each jar. Keep jars upright at all times to avoid getting food into sealing area of lids. Add more hot water, if needed, pouring around jars, not directly onto them, so water level is 1 to 2 inches above jars.

2. Cover canner with lid and bring to a vigorous boil. Periodically open lid to make sure water is at least 1 inch above jars. If not, add more boiling water. Total boiling time varies by recipe but is typically around 15 minutes.

3. Turn off heat and let jars rest, undisturbed, for 5 minutes so food contents can settle.

4. Use a jar lifter to remove 1 jar at a time, taking care to keep each upright. Place jars on a clean towel with plenty of room between each so they cool evenly. Make sure jars are not in a cold draft like in front of an air conditioner or breezy window. Extreme changes in temperature can cause the jars to crack.

5. Within a few minutes, you should hear a "ping" each time a jar lid seals. If you do not hear "pings," the jars did not properly seal. Use the contents of those unsealed jars right away or refrigerate them for up to one week, but do not store them unrefrigerated (contents will spoil).* Let the properly sealed jars cool at room temperature, undisturbed, for 24 hours.

6. Rinse jars, including lids, to remove any food residue. Label each with date and store in a cool, dry place out of direct light for up to 1 year.

* If you ever open a jar that smells off-putting, do not eat it. Improperly canned foods can carry harmful bacteria.

BREAD & BUTTER PICKLES

There are two kinds of people: those who like dills, and those who like bread and butter pickles. I like both.

You can find pickling cucumbers almost anywhere you find regular salad cucumbers. They are bred specifically for pickling, so they will be more crisp and flavorful when pickled.

Makes 4 quarts

Song: Come on in My Kitchen, Robert Johnson

25 pickling cucumbers,
    cut in 1/4-inch slices
6 red onions, thinly sliced
8 cloves garlic, chopped
1/2 cup kosher salt
3 cups apple cider vinegar
5 cups sugar
1 1/2 teaspoons celery seed
1/2 teaspoon whole cloves
1 tablespoon ground turmeric
4 glass quart jars, sterilized,
    if preserving

In a large nonreactive bowl, combine cucumbers, onions, garlic, and salt. Set aside to macerate for 3 hours. Drain and discard accumulated liquid from vegetables.

In a large nonreactive saucepan, combine vinegar, sugar, celery seed, cloves, and turmeric, and bring to a boil. Add drained vegetables and boil for 30 seconds. Remove from heat.

If preserving, divide cucumbers and canning liquid between each jar, leaving 1/4-inch headspace. Follow preserving instructions on page 77. Boil cucumber-filled jars in the hot water bath for 10 minutes.

If not preserving, allow pickles to cool completely and refrigerate for up to 1 week in canning liquid.

REFRIGERATOR PICKLES

The difference between refrigerator pickles and canning pickles? Refrigerator pickles are not processed in a hot-water bath or meant to be stored for a long time. They keep beautifully in the fridge for a week or so. We use this method with our pickles at Auntie Em's because we go through them so quickly. This recipe is a little spicy, a little dilly, and not too sweet. They became so popular at the restaurant that we now pack them in pints for sale.

Makes 4 pints

4 cups cider vinegar

4 tablespoons sugar

2 tablespoons kosher salt

1 teaspoon celery seed

12 Kirby cucumbers, sliced in 1/4-inch chips

8 garlic cloves

4 sprigs dill

4 dried chiles de árbol

2 teaspoons mustard seed, divided

4 glass pint jars, sterilized, if preserving

Song: All Your Love, Otis Rush

In a medium nonreactive saucepan, bring vinegar, sugar, and salt to boil. Reduce heat to medium and gently boil until sugar is dissolved, about 5 minutes.

Meanwhile, divide cucumber chips evenly between jars. Wedge 2 garlic cloves, 1 dill sprig, and 1 chile between cucumbers and side of each jar so they are visible through glass. Top each jar with 1/2 teaspoon mustard seed.

Divide hot brine between each jar. Allow pickles to cool to room temperature before securing with lids. Refrigerate for up to 1 week, or preserve according to the directions on page 77.

SPICY PICKLED BEETS

I'm a big fan of pickled vegetables on a cheese platter. Pickled beets go very well with the tang of a goat cheese. You can use these in an apple, beet, and goat cheese salad, or an arugula, pickled beet, and ricotta salata salad. In general, pair these beets with creamy cheeses that have peppery, tangy, and/or sweet flavors.

Makes 2 quarts

2 pounds baby beets, peeled and quartered
3 tablespoons plus 2 teaspoons kosher salt
1 cup red wine vinegar
3/4 cup sugar
1 small red onion, sliced into
  1/4-inch rounds

4 garlic cloves, peeled
5 red chiles, such as chile de árbol,
  roughly chopped
2 bay leaves
2 4-inch stalks of dill
2 glass quart jars, sterilized, if preserving

In a large nonreactive pot, combine beets with 2 teaspoons salt. Add enough cold water to just cover beets and bring to a boil over high heat. Reduce heat to medium and simmer until beets are barely tender but still firm, about 8 minutes. Take care not to overcook— they should not get soft. Drain beets, reserving 4 cups of cooking liquid.

Pour reserved cooking liquid back into pot and add remaining 3 tablespoons salt, vinegar, and sugar. Bring to a boil and cook until sugar is dissolved, about 1 minute. Pour pickling liquid into a medium bowl and cool completely.

Meanwhile, alternately layer beets, onions, garlic, and chiles in each jar. Wedge a bay leaf and dill stalk between beets and side of each jar so they are visible through glass.

If preserving, divide cooled canning liquid between jars, leaving 1/4-inch headspace. Follow preserving instructions on page 77. Boil beet-filled jars in the hot water bath for 10 minutes.

If not preserving, refrigerate beets for at least 4 days in canning liquid to allow flavors to develop. Refrigerate for up to 1 month.

Song: Knocked Out Cold, Action Swingers

The Auntie Em's Cookbook

DILLY BEANS

These beans are great edible stirrers and garnishes for Bloody Marys.

Makes 4 pints

1 pound green beans
1 pound wax beans
8 cloves garlic, peeled
4 sprigs fresh dill
1/2 teaspoon crushed red pepper flakes
1 1/4 cups apple cider vinegar
1 1/4 cups white wine vinegar
1/4 cup kosher salt
4 glass pint jars, sterilized, if preserving

Song: Something's Got a Hold of Me, Etta James

Trim beans 1 inch shorter than height of jars. Divide green and wax beans evenly among jars. Wedge 2 cloves garlic between beans and side of each jar so garlic is visible through glass. Repeat with dill. Top each jar with 1/8 teaspoon crushed red pepper.

Meanwhile, in a medium nonreactive pot, bring vinegars, salt, and 2 1/2 cups water to a boil. Remove from heat. If preserving, divide beans and canning liquid between each jar, leaving 1/4-inch headspace. Follow preserving instructions on page 77. Boil bean-filled jars in the hot water bath for 10 minutes.

If not preserving, allow to cool completely and refrigerate for up to 1 week in canning liquid.

REACTIVE VS. NONREACTIVE COOKWARE

A reactive pan contains aluminum, cast iron, or unlined copper. While these materials conduct heat very well and are ideal for cooking rice, melting sugar, and pan-browning meat, they react with acidic foods, such as tomato sauce, and the metal can alter the color and flavor of the dish. Stainless steel is the best nonreactive metal to use with acidic foods.

Quick Heirloom Tomato Sauce

This recipe is a must for your end-of-summer tomatoes—the ones you don't know what to do with because they're all ripe at once and need to be used in a day. Or the ones that are so cheap at the farmers' market because the farmers have so many.

I often get what are called No. 2 tomatoes from the farmers to make this sauce. No. 2s are just fine to eat but may be oddly shaped or have a blemish, so they're sold at a discount. Get to know your farmer and ask him or her to save you the No. 2s.

This sauce can be frozen, canned, or refrigerated. It's great to have on hand for soups, stews, curries, or pasta sauce. This is another recipe that is easy to multiply if you have more tomatoes.

Makes 2 quarts

1/2 cup extra-virgin olive oil
5 pounds very ripe heirloom tomatoes, roughly chopped
6 cloves garlic, minced
4 teaspoons red pepper flakes
2 teaspoons sugar
2 teaspoons sea salt
1 tablespoon basil chiffonade
1 teaspoon thyme leaves
1 teaspoon oregano leaves
Sea salt and freshly ground pepper
2 glass quart jars, sterilized, if preserving

In a large nonreactive pot, heat olive oil over high heat. Add tomatoes and sauté for 4 minutes, stirring occasionally so tomatoes remain well-coated in oil. Add garlic, red pepper flakes, sugar, and salt. Bring to a boil, reduce heat to medium, and simmer for 7 minutes, stirring occasionally. Add basil, thyme, and oregano, stir well, and remove from heat.

Allow tomato sauce to cool slightly and purée in a food processor until smooth.

Song: Sugar Sugar, Jimmy Reed

If preserving, divide hot sauce between each jar, leaving 1/4-inch headspace. Follow preserving instructions on page 77. Boil sauce-filled jars in the hot water bath for 15 minutes.

If not preserving, allow sauce to cool completely and refrigerate for up to 1 week, or transfer individual portions to freezer bags or freezer-safe plastic containers. Freeze for up to 2 months.

OVEN-DRIED TOMATOES IN OLIVE OIL

Oven-dried tomatoes are nice to use on a BLT to pack a little extra flavor punch. These tomatoes will keep nicely in the refrigerator for up to two weeks. You can easily multiply the quantity if you have more tomatoes.

Makes about 2 pints, varies depending on tomato type

4 pounds plum tomatoes,
   sliced in half lengthwise
6 cloves garlic, thinly sliced
6 sprigs thyme, leaves only
6 tablespoons extra-virgin olive oil
2 teaspoons sea salt
1 teaspoon freshly ground pepper

Preheat oven to 200°.

Place tomatoes, cut side up, on a baking sheet. Sprinkle garlic and thyme over tomatoes and drizzle with olive oil. Sprinkle with salt and pepper.

Roast tomatoes until dried but still plump, about 7 hours. Allow to cool completely and pack into an airtight container. Refrigerate for up to 2 weeks.

Song: Bourgeois Blues, Lead Belly

SPICY KETCHUP

This ketchup is a staple at Auntie Em's. It goes great with the Herb-roasted Breakfast Potatoes on page 112.

Makes 2 quarts

3 pounds very ripe tomatoes,
 roughly chopped
1 1/2 teaspoons extra-virgin olive oil
1/2 cup shallots, minced
2 cloves garlic, minced
1/4 cup brown sugar
1/2 teaspoon mustard powder

1/2 teaspoon ground ginger
1/4 teaspoon crushed red pepper
1/4 teaspoon finely chopped chile de árbol
1/4 teaspoon ground allspice
1/8 teaspoon ground cloves
1/4 cup apple cider vinegar
1 tablespoon sea salt, more to taste
2 glass quart jars, sterilized, if preserving

In a blender, purée tomatoes until smooth. Strain tomato purée through a sieve. Set aside.

In a medium nonreactive saucepan, heat oil over medium-high heat. Add shallots and garlic, reduce heat to medium, and sauté until vegetables are soft, about 4 minutes. Add tomatoes, brown sugar, mustard powder, ginger, red pepper, chile, allspice, and cloves. Reduce heat to low and simmer until thickened, about 45 minutes, stirring occasionally. Add vinegar and salt and simmer until mixture is consistency of ketchup, about 30 minutes. Season with additional salt to taste.

If preserving, divide ketchup between each jar, leaving 1/4-inch headspace. Follow preserving instructions on page 77. Boil ketchup-filled jars in the hot water bath for 15 minutes.

If not preserving, allow ketchup to cool completely and refrigerate for up to 1 week.

Song: Brown Sugar, The Rolling Stones

Green Tomato & Zucchini Chow Chow

A traditional Southern chow chow calls for bell peppers, but they're one of the only foods on earth I don't like, so I make mine with jalapeños. I like the little bit of bite they add.

This recipe is a great way to use end-of-summer vegetables from the garden and farmers' market. When preserved, it makes enough to last you through the winter. Use chow chow on chicken, fish, and egg dishes—it adds a ton of flavor. Note that you need to brine the main ingredients a day in advance.

Makes 4 pints

1/4 cup sea salt, more to taste
2 cups cored green tomatoes, chopped into 1-inch cubes (about 2 medium)
2 cups zucchini, chopped into 1-inch cubes (about 2 medium)
1 cup yellow onions, chopped into 1/2-inch cubes (about 1 medium)
1 cup minced celery (about 2 medium stalks)
2 jalapeños, seeded and thinly sliced

FOR COOKING LIQUID:
2 cups white wine vinegar
1 cup sugar
1 tablespoon ground turmeric
1 tablespoon celery seed
2 bay leaves
1 teaspoon cloves
1 teaspoon ground allspice
1 teaspoon freshly ground pepper, more to taste
2 tablespoons finely chopped parsley
2 tablespoons finely chopped cilantro
4 glass pint jars, sterilized, if preserving

Song: Jelly Roll Blues, Jelly Roll Morton

In a large bowl, combine 4 cups water and salt. Stir to dissolve salt. Add tomatoes, zucchini, onions, celery, and jalapeños to brine. Cover and refrigerate overnight.

Drain vegetables and place in a large, heavy-bottomed pot.

In a medium bowl, combine vinegar, 1 cup water, sugar, turmeric, celery seed, bay leaves, cloves, allspice, and pepper. Mix well and add to vegetable mixture.

Bring vegetable mixture to a boil, reduce heat, and simmer until vegetables are tender, about 40 minutes. Taste and season with additional salt and pepper to taste. Stir in parsley and cilantro.

If preserving, allow to cool 15 minutes and divide hot chow chow and canning liquid between each jar, leaving 1/4-inch headspace. Follow preserving instructions on page 77. Boil chow chow-filled jars in the hot water bath for 15 minutes.

If not preserving, allow chow chow to cool for 12 hours at room temperature. Refrigerate for up to 1 week.

LAURA ANN'S BLUEBERRY BASIL JAM

I love my friend Laura Ann's jam on grilled chicken. It's a lovely combination of sweet and savory, and it screams of summer. Note that while quite simple to make, it's a two-day process, so plan ahead.

If you'd like to sample some of Laura Ann's other amazing jams, check out her site, www.lauraannsjams.com.

Makes 6 8-ounce jars

6 cups (3 pints) organic blueberries
Juice and zest of 1 lemon
7 cups organic sugar
1 bunch (about 1 1/2 cups) organic basil (whole, stems and all)
6 8-ounce glass jars, sterilized

Gently rinse blueberries and drain in a colander. Pour into a ceramic bowl and add sugar, lemon juice, and lemon zest. Lightly rinse the basil (stems and all) and give it a good spanking—take the basil in your hands and give it a good slap or two. You're getting the natural oils out—it's a bartender trick. Gently mix basil into blueberry mixture. Set aside to macerate for 1 hour.

Transfer to a large pot and bring mixture to a boil. Cook for 5 minutes, then transfer back into the ceramic bowl. Let cool, cover, and store overnight in the fridge.

The next day, remove the basil. The flavor will remain after the leaves and stems are gone. Place berry mixture in a large pot and bring to a slow boil. When it's at a full boil, continue to cook it for 5 to 10 minutes until you get the consistency you like. I usually "test the set" by putting a small spoonful of the mixture on a plate, letting it cool a bit, and seeing if it has the set that I like. You can also use a candy thermometer—the setting point is about 220°.

When the mixture has set, remove from heat and follow the directions on page 77 to can the jam.

Song: C Jam Blues, Duke Ellington

The Auntie Em's Cookbook

Pesto is a handy little thing to have around the kitchen to flavor so many dishes. I stir it into soups, use it in pastas and rice, and spread it onto sandwiches. At the end of summer, I strip all my remaining basil plants of their leaves, which tend to be a bit tougher than the leaves at the beginning of the season. This makes them perfect for pesto. I freeze the pesto in ice cube trays, pop out the cubes, and put them in a plastic freezer bag. Now I have frozen cubes of deliciousness to use throughout the fall and winter.

I find that using only olive oil in pesto can be a little strong. I like to use half extra-virgin olive oil and half vegetable oil, so it's not quite as assertive, but you can adjust as you prefer.

Makes 2 cups

3 cups basil leaves
1 1/4 cups grated parmesan,
    preferably Parmigiano Reggiano, divided
1/4 cup pine nuts
1/2 cup extra-virgin olive oil
1/2 cup vegetable oil
1 teaspoon sea salt, more to taste
1/2 teaspoon freshly ground pepper, more to taste

In food processor, combine basil, parmesan, and pine nuts. Slowly drizzle in both oils while pulsing the processor. Continue to pulse until pesto is almost smooth but retains a slightly chunky texture. Transfer to a medium bowl and stir in salt and pepper. Season with additional salt and pepper to taste. Refrigerate for up to 1 week or freeze.

Song: Pretty Thing, Bo Diddley

Fall

FALL

Pear & Ginger Baked French Toast

Pumpkin Pancakes with Persimmons & Pecans

Fig, Blue Cheese & Prosciutto Tartine

Spicy Pimiento Cheese & Bacon Tartine

Andouille Sausage & Shrimp Scramble

Fennel, Tomato & Parmesan Salad with Poached Eggs

Fried Green Tomatoes & Eggs

Braised Pork with Greens & Eggs

Roasted Mushroom Grits & Poached Eggs

Brussels Sprouts & Potato Hash with Poached Eggs

Herb-roasted Breakfast Potatoes

Double Garlic Greens

Curried Chickpea Salad

Pear & Cranberry Compote

WHAT'S IN SEASON IN FALL?

Apples	Curly endive	Onions
Artichokes	(frisee)	Parsnips
Arugula	Edamame	Pears
Beets	Eggplant	Peppers
Belgian endive	Fennel	Persimmons
Broccoli	Figs	Pomegranates
Broccoli rabe	Garlic	Potatoes
Brussels sprouts	Grapes	Pumpkins
Cabbage	Horseradish	Radicchio
Carrots	Kale	Spinach
Cauliflower	Kohlrabi	Sunchokes
Celery	Lettuces	Sweet potatoes
Chard	Limes	Tomatillos
Chicory	Mushrooms	Turnips
Cranberries	Okra	Winter squash

Pumpkins, Persimmons, Figs & Slow-roasted Pork, Oh My!

Oh, fall in Los Angeles! How I love you. Bright and sunny, but cool days. A little rain; a bit of wind to blow the dust of summer away. It's time to put away the dresses and flip-flops and get out the combat boots and sweaters! I put my rugs back on the hardwood floors to catch the dirt and mud from the dogs' paws.

In the garden, I rip out the tomato, zucchini, and basil plants and start the lettuces, broccoli, cauliflower, and winter squashes. My garden beds get a huge dose of chicken poop, spent hay, new compost, and a couple of weeks' breather from pumping out veggies.

The baby chickens that arrived in spring are now fully grown and laying small blue, brown, and white eggs. As they get older, their eggs get bigger. The summer was spent teaching them to lay eggs in their nests and not on the ground in their run. They have an odd habit of all wanting to lay in the same place, instead of in their own nests. Some mornings, I've walked into their house to collect eggs and all fifteen eggs were on two nests. I've learned that if I leave a single egg on each of the nests, it encourages them to lay their eggs on all of the nests.

The beginning of fall also finds Charles in the yard repairing the coop. He puts up new netting overhead so the girls can't fly out and the hawks can't fly in. By now, my older chickens have molted and have beautiful, warm new feathers. I collect the fallen feathers to use in fall flower arrangements.

The farmers' markets are now moving on from the thousands of pounds of heavenly heirloom tomatoes that took up all of their real estate and making way for hard squashes, gourds, and pumpkins. Our summer scramble at Auntie Em's turns into a fall scramble of butternut squash, spinach, and goat fromage blanc. We ramp up for Thanksgiving pies. The seasonal scones and muffins change flavors, using figs, apples, and persimmons.

Over the span of one short week, we stop cooling the restaurant and start heating it up for our bakers and cooks, who work late nights and early mornings. The front and back patios lose the umbrellas and gain heaters. There's nothing better than walking into Auntie Em's early in the morning on a chilly fall day to the aroma of Noah's croissants in the oven.

Some of my favorite fall flavors are pumpkin, persimmons, figs, and slow-roasted pork. You'll find them all in the pages ahead. Yum.

Pear & Ginger Baked French Toast

Pear and ginger are one of those perfect flavor combinations—a classic for a reason. I love to serve this on a chilly fall morning.

Serves 6

For the batter:

1 tablespoon honey
1 tablespoon orange juice
1/2 teaspoon ground cinnamon
1/4 teaspoon ground ginger
1 cup heavy cream
3 large eggs

Heat honey in microwave for 10 seconds to thin. In a medium bowl, whisk together honey, orange juice, cinnamon, ginger, cream, and eggs. Set aside.

For the french toast:

3 tablespoons honey
3 large ripe pears, cored, peeled, and thinly sliced
2 tablespoons finely minced fresh ginger
6 to 8 pieces brioche or similar bread, sliced about 2 inches thick

Pure maple syrup, for serving

Preheat oven to 350°.

Grease (nonstick spray or butter) a 9″ × 13″ baking dish. Heat honey in microwave for 10 seconds and pour into baking dish. Set aside.

In a medium bowl, toss pears with ginger. Arrange pears in layers on top of honey. Arrange bread slices on top of pears. Pour batter over bread and press down gently to make sure slices are all covered in batter.

Bake until the top is golden brown and the egg mixture is set, about 35 to 40 minutes. Serve immediately with maple syrup.

The Auntie Em's Cookbook

Song: Real Smiles, White Fence

Pumpkin Pancakes with Persimmons & Pecans

This recipe calls for canned pumpkin, which is more consistent than fresh pumpkin. Not to mention much easier.

Makes 8 4-inch pancakes

For persimmons:

2 tablespoons butter
5 Fuyu persimmons, diced into 1-inch pieces
1 teaspoon pure maple syrup
1 teaspoon vanilla extract
1/4 teaspoon cinnamon
1/8 teaspoon sea salt

In a medium nonstick sauté pan, melt butter over medium heat. When butter begins to sizzle, add persimmons, maple syrup, vanilla, cinnamon, and salt. Sauté until persimmons soften and are completely coated in sauce, about 5 minutes. Set aside.

For pecans:

3 tablespoons unsalted pecans, roughly chopped

Preheat oven to 350°. Place pecans on a baking sheet and bake until toasted and fragrant, about 5 minutes. Set aside.

For cinnamon whipped cream:

1 cup heavy cream
1/4 cup confectioners' sugar
1/2 teaspoon cinnamon
1/4 teaspoon vanilla extract

In a medium bowl or stand mixer, combine cream, powdered sugar, cinnamon, and vanilla and beat with a hand mixer or whisk attachment until stiff peaks form, about 3 minutes. Cover and place in refrigerator until ready to use, up to 4 hours.

FOR PANCAKES:

1 1/4 cups flour

2 1/2 tablespoons sugar

2 teaspoons baking powder

1/2 teaspoon cinnamon

1/2 teaspoon ground ginger

1/2 teaspoon nutmeg

1/2 teaspoon sea salt

1 cup whole milk

6 tablespoons canned pumpkin

3 tablespoons unsalted butter, melted, plus 2 to 3 tablespoons (not melted), divided

1 large egg

In a medium bowl, whisk together flour, sugar, baking powder, cinnamon, ginger, nutmeg, and salt.

In a large bowl, whisk together milk, pumpkin, melted butter, and egg. With a rubber spatula, fold wet ingredients into dry ingredients. Mix until well combined.

In a large frying pan or flat-top grill, melt 1 1/2 tablespoons butter. Pour 1/3 cup batter into pan for each pancake. You should be able to fit 4 to 6 pancakes, depending on the size of your pan. Cook until pancakes are golden brown on the bottom, about 2 to 3 minutes after bubbles begin to form in the center. Flip and cook until a knife or toothpick inserted in the center comes out clean, about 2 to 3 minutes. Total cooking time is 5 to 6 minutes. Transfer pancakes to a plate and repeat with remaining butter and batter, adding more butter as needed.

To serve, top pancakes with sautéed persimmons, toasted pecans, and a dollop of cinnamon whipped cream. Serve immediately.

Song: The Thrill of it All, Roxy Music

Fig, Blue Cheese & Prosciutto Tartine

The floral sweetness of figs paired with the tang of blue cheese and the salty savoriness of prosciutto make for a perfect flavor combination. In season from June through early fall, figs have a delicate skin and a juicy, soft, velvety inside. They won't ripen once they're picked, so make sure you choose ripe ones. You know they're ripe if they feel heavy for their size and have a floral, honey smell at the stem. I love Black Mission figs, but you can always use Brown Turkeys or Calimyrnas, which are a beautiful pale green color.

Makes 4 tartines

4 tablespoons Blue Cheese Spread
  (*see recipe below*)
4 slices ciabatta bread
Leaves from 2 sprigs thyme
4 thin slices prosciutto

8 figs, such as Black Mission or
  Brown Turkey
1/4 cup roughly chopped hazelnuts,
  toasted

Spread 1 tablespoon Blue Cheese Spread on a slice of ciabatta bread. Repeat on the remaining 3 slices. Sprinkle thyme leaves evenly over the 4 slices of bread. Top each slice with a piece of prosciutto.

Slice the figs in half lengthwise. Arrange 4 fig slices atop the prosciutto on each tartine. Sprinkle with toasted hazelnuts. Serve immediately.

Blue Cheese Spread

This recipe will make more than you need for the tartines. Store leftovers in an airtight container in the refrigerator.

Makes 8 ounces

4 ounces cream cheese, room temperature
4 ounces quality blue cheese (such as Point Reyes Blue), crumbled and well chilled
Sea salt and freshly ground pepper

In a medium bowl, combine cream cheese and blue cheese. Stir to incorporate, taking care to leave the blue cheese chunky. Season with salt and pepper to taste. Refrigerate for up to 1 week.

SPICY PIMIENTO CHEESE & BACON TARTINE

I once visited a friend's family in Jasper, Georgia. His mom brought out a container of homemade pimiento cheese spread and white bread for lunch. Not being from the South, I was hesitant, needless to say. But I tried it, and from that day on I was hooked. We sat on the back porch, ate the sandwiches, and sipped whiskey cocktails. We make the cheese spread for specials at Auntie Em's and sell containers of it in the cheese case during the holidays.

Makes 4 tartines

4 slices good-quality white sandwich bread
8 tablespoons Pimiento Cheese Spread (*recipe below*)
8 slices applewood-smoked bacon, cooked crispy

Toast bread and place on 4 plates. Spread 2 tablespoons cheese spread on each slice and top with bacon. Serve immediately.

PIMIENTO CHEESE SPREAD
1 1/2 cups good-quality mayonnaise
1 pound good-quality sharp cheddar cheese, shredded
1 4-ounce jar pimientos, drained
1 teaspoon Worcestershire sauce
1 teaspoon grated onion
1/2 teaspoon sea salt
1/2 teaspoon freshly ground pepper

In a food processor, combine all ingredients and pulse several times until just combined. Do not over-process—you should see separate cheese and pimiento pieces.

Song: Satisfy You, The Seeds

ANDOUILLE SAUSAGE & SHRIMP SCRAMBLE

The Monterey Bay Aquarium's Seafood Watch (www.seafoodwatch.org) is a great tool to use for making sustainable seafood choices; they even have a smartphone app that you can consult when you're at a fish counter or reading a menu. Check the guide for your area to find the type of shrimp that's best to use.

This dish pairs really well with the Herb-roasted Breakfast Potatoes on page 112.

Serves 4 to 6

1 tablespoon unsalted butter
1 medium red bell pepper, seeded and diced into 1/2-inch pieces
1/2 medium onion, diced in 1/2-inch pieces
1 pound andouille sausage, sliced into 1/2-inch coins
1 tablespoon Creole seasoning
1 teaspoon fresh thyme leaves
1/2 pound medium shrimp, cleaned, shelled, and roughly chopped
10 large eggs
1/2 cup heavy cream
1/2 cup scallions, green parts only, finely chopped
Sea salt and freshly ground pepper

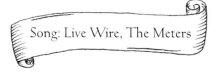
Song: Live Wire, The Meters

In a large skillet, melt butter over medium-high heat. Add red pepper and onion and sauté until translucent, about 4 minutes. Add sausage, Creole seasoning, and thyme. Sauté until sausage begins to brown, about 3 minutes. Add shrimp and sauté until shrimp turns white, about 2 minutes.

Meanwhile, in a large bowl, whisk together eggs and cream. When shrimp is cooked, add egg mixture to skillet and reduce heat to medium-low. Slowly stir every few minutes as eggs begin to firm up, about 5 minutes. Remove from heat. Do not overcook the eggs; they should be slightly runny. They will continue to cook when off the flame.

Divide eggs between 4 plates, sprinkle with scallions, and season with salt and pepper to taste. Serve immediately.

FENNEL, TOMATO & PARMESAN SALAD WITH POACHED EGGS

This salad is perfect for those end-of-summer tomatoes. They taste terrific with the runny yolk of a poached egg and sea salt. I use a mandoline to slice the fennel paper-thin. The bitter greens are fantastic with the lemon in the dressing and the sweetness of the tomatoes.

Serves 6

4 large heirloom tomatoes (about 1 pound), diced into 1/2-inch pieces
1 large fennel bulb, sliced very thin
4 cups mixed baby greens, such as arugula, chicory, radicchio, and/or beet greens
1/2 cup shaved parmesan, preferably Parmigiano Reggiano
2 1/2 tablespoons extra-virgin olive oil
2 tablespoons fresh lemon juice
1 teaspoon sea salt, more to taste
1/2 teaspoon freshly ground pepper, more to taste
6 large eggs

In a large bowl, toss together tomatoes, fennel, greens, parmesan, olive oil, and lemon juice. Add salt and pepper, toss again, and refrigerate while making the eggs.

Follow directions on page 191 for poaching eggs.

Divide salad between 6 plates and top each with a poached egg. Sprinkle each egg with a pinch of salt and pepper. Serve immediately.

Song: Salad Days, Minor Threat

FRIED GREEN TOMATOES & EGGS

This is a great use for those last unripe green tomatoes before they get pulled from the garden to make room for your fall planting. You can also get green tomatoes at the farmers' market. Of course, there's a difference between an heirloom tomato that's green when ripe, like the Green Zebra or Aunt Ruby's German Green, and a plain, old unripe tomato. You want the latter for this recipe. Because they are still very firm, they hold up well to frying, plus they have a nice tang. I slice the tomatoes thick to give them meatiness.

You can also use these fried green tomatoes on a BLT instead of ripe red tomatoes, or as an appetizer served with a homemade ranch dressing.

Serves 4

2 large eggs, lightly beaten
1/2 cup whole milk
2 teaspoons sea salt, divided
1 cup flour
1 cup cornmeal
1 teaspoon cayenne pepper
1 teaspoon freshly ground pepper
4 large green, unripe tomatoes, sliced into 1/2-inch thick slices
1/2 cup vegetable oil, divided, or as needed
8 eggs, scrambled
2 teaspoons finely chopped chives
Sea salt and freshly ground pepper

In a medium bowl, whisk together eggs, milk, and 1 teaspoon salt. In a small bowl, combine flour and 1/2 teaspoon salt. In another small bowl, mix together cornmeal, remaining 1/2 teaspoon salt, cayenne, and pepper. Mix all together well.

Dip tomatoes first in flour mixture, then egg mixture, and finally dredge in cornmeal mixture.

In a large skillet, heat 1/4 cup oil over medium-high heat. Add breaded tomatoes, 4 to 5 at a time, or as many that will fit will in pan without touching. Cook until tomatoes begin to brown on the bottom, about 3 minutes. Flip and brown on other side, 2 to 3 minutes. Drain on paper towels and set aside. Repeat with remaining tomatoes.

Scramble eggs in a medium skillet; follow the advice on page 190 if you need guidance.

Arrange 4 tomatoes on each of 4 plates in a slightly overlapping fan pattern. Place scrambled eggs directly on top of fried tomatoes. Sprinkle with chives and season with salt and pepper to taste. Serve immediately.

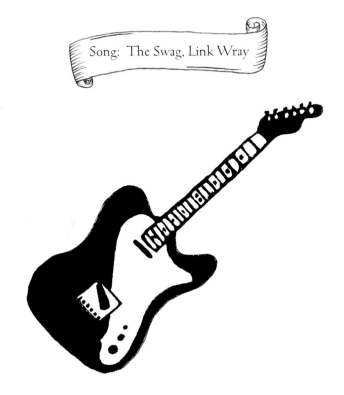

Song: The Swag, Link Wray

BRAISED PORK WITH GREENS & EGGS

The South has inspired my cooking more than anywhere else I've traveled. To me, Southern food is humble, delicious, and real. Pork butt (also referred to as pork shoulder) is generally an inexpensive piece of meat and a Southern staple. It takes a long time to make. You have to cook it slow and low to melt away the tough connective tissue and fat, which leaves you with an insanely tasty and moist piece of meat. This dish screams cold-weather comfort food.

You'll have leftovers after braising a whole pork butt; I use them for tacos, burritos, pork chili, and curry.

To make this dish really sing, top the pork with Warm Tomatillo Salsa, which you'll find on page 192.

Serves 4, with lots of leftover pork

1/4 cup smoked paprika

1/8 cup freshly ground pepper, more to
taste

2 tablespoons garlic powder

1 tablespoon onion powder

1 tablespoon cayenne

1/4 cup sea salt, more to taste

1 tablespoon brown sugar

1 4-pound pork butt

2 tablespoons vegetable oil

1/2 bottle red wine, such as Cabernet

2 cups good-quality beef or chicken stock

4 sprigs thyme

2 3-inch sprigs rosemary

2 bay leaves

1 medium onion, quartered

1 carrot, peeled and quartered

3 stalks celery, roughly chopped

8 cloves garlic, peeled

Double Garlic Greens (*see recipe page 113*)

8 eggs, scrambled

BRAISING TIPS

Make sure to get a nice sear on your pork butt. Dry the pork well with paper towels before seasoning it and get the cast iron skillet very hot. (You want to caramelize the pork rather than steam it. If wet, it will create steam.) The caramelized skin creates a great layer of flavor.

And do not pick at your pork once it is covered and cooking! That lets out the moisture that keeps the meat tender.

Song: I Want You, The Troggs

Preheat oven to 300°.

In a medium bowl, combine paprika, pepper, garlic and onion powders, cayenne, salt, and brown sugar. Pat pork butt dry with paper towels and coat with spice mixture. Set aside.

In a large cast iron skillet, heat oil over high heat. Add pork butt and sear on all sides until golden brown.

Transfer pork to a large Dutch oven. Add wine, stock, thyme and rosemary sprigs, bay leaves, onion, carrots, celery, and garlic. Cover pork with foil and place lid on Dutch oven (adjust foil so steam does not escape). Place in oven and braise for 4 hours. Do not open the lid.

Remove pork from oven and transfer carefully from pot to a rimmed baking sheet. Set aside until cool enough to handle, about 15 to 20 minutes. Pull off small pieces of meat (it should shred in your fingers). Season with salt and pepper to taste and serve immediately with Double Garlic Greens (page 113) and scrambled eggs (page 190).

TO MAKE A STOCK FOR SOUPS OR STEWS:
When the pork braising liquid is cool, remove the vegetables and skim the fat. Strain and refrigerate or freeze.

ROASTED MUSHROOM GRITS & POACHED EGGS

When the Red Aunts toured the South, and we played Atlanta, we'd go to a place for Sunday brunch called Mary Mac's Tea Room, which has been there since 1945. It's a rather large place that fills up with the after-church crowd in their Sunday finest—but we'd walk in hungover and wearing scrappy clothes, with our set lists from the night before still written in black Sharpie on our arms. We were still welcomed. Mary Mac's is about traditional Southern food: fried chicken, collards, fried oysters, okra, mac and cheese, and really good grits. I loved those grits.

Today, we do grits a couple of different ways at Auntie Em's. This is one of the recipes, inspired by my memories of Mary Mac's.

You can find stone-ground grits at well-stocked grocery stores (do not use quick grits) and directly from many Southern farmers online. Truffle cheese is available from Cowgirl Creamery, well-stocked grocery stores, and most cheese shops.

Serves 4

1 1/2 cups oyster mushrooms, cleaned and stems removed
1 1/2 cups shiitake mushrooms, cleaned and stems removed
1/4 cup extra-virgin olive oil
5 sprigs thyme, leaves only
5 cloves garlic, minced
1 1/2 teaspoons sea salt, divided, more to taste
1 teaspoon freshly ground pepper, more to taste
2 cups whole milk
2 cups water
1 teaspoon freshly ground pepper
1 cup stone-ground grits
2 tablespoons unsalted butter
2 ounces truffle cheese, such as Truffle Tremor (Cypress Grove Creamery) or Sottocenere al tartufo
4 poached eggs (*see instructions page 191*)
1 tablespoon chives, finely chopped

Preheat oven to 400°.

Roughly chop oyster and shiitake mushrooms the size of a nickel. In a medium bowl, mix together mushrooms, olive oil, thyme, garlic, 1 teaspoon salt, and pepper. Spread mushrooms on a rimmed baking sheet and roast until golden brown, about 20 minutes.

While mushrooms are roasting, prepare the grits. In a large saucepan, combine milk, water, 1/2 teaspoon salt, and pepper. Bring to a boil, reduce heat to low, and add grits 1/4 cup at a time, whisking constantly, until fully combined. Cook on medium-low heat, stirring occasionally, until creamy and smooth, about 15 minutes. Remove from heat. Add butter and cheese and mix well. Stir in mushrooms.

Follow the recipe on page 191 to make poached eggs.

Divide grits evenly among 4 bowls. Top each with a poached egg, pinch of chives, and season with salt and pepper to taste. Serve immediately.

Song: Girls Ain't Groceries, Little Milton

A jam session with the girls

BRUSSELS SPROUTS & POTATO HASH WITH POACHED EGGS

I inherited my love for brussels sprouts from my dad. They are my favorite cruciferous vegetable.

A TIP: Rinsing the potatoes after you dice them will remove some of the excess starch so they get crispy.

Serves 4

2 tablespoons extra-virgin olive oil
8 medium fingerling potatoes, chopped into 1-inch pieces and rinsed
1/2 pound brussels sprouts, finely chopped
5 sage leaves, roughly chopped
1 teaspoon sea salt, more to taste
1 teaspoon freshly ground pepper, more to taste
4 poached eggs (*see instructions page 191*)

In a medium sauté pan, heat olive oil over medium-high heat. Add potatoes and brussels sprouts and sprinkle with sage, salt, and pepper. Sauté for 1 minute, then turn heat down to medium. Shake pan gently or use a spatula to flip vegetables. Sauté until potatoes and brussels sprouts are golden brown on the bottom, about 6 minutes. Flip again, and sauté until tender and golden brown with crispy brown edges, about 8 TO 10 minutes. Set aside.

Follow the recipe on page 191 for the perfect poached eggs.

Divide hash between 4 plates, top each with a poached egg, and season with salt and pepper to taste. Serve immediately.

Song: Red Hot Mama, Parliament

HERB-ROASTED BREAKFAST POTATOES

These super-flavorful potatoes are perfect with any egg dish. They are especially good with my homemade ketchup on page 85.

Serves 4

2 pounds fingerling potatoes, sliced into 1/2-inch coins
1/4 cup extra-virgin olive oil
1 tablespoon fresh thyme leaves
1 tablespoon finely chopped fresh rosemary
1 tablespoon finely chopped fresh dill
3 cloves garlic, minced
1 tablespoon sea salt, more to taste
1 1/2 teaspoons freshly ground pepper, more to taste

Song: Potato, Tyvek

Preheat oven to 375°.

In a medium bowl, toss together all ingredients. Spread out potatoes evenly on a large rimmed baking sheet so most do not touch. Roast until potatoes are tender and the edges are crispy, about 30 to 40 minutes. Season with additional salt and pepper to taste and serve immediately.

DOUBLE GARLIC GREENS

I love greens! Collards, mustard, turnip greens, beet greens, kale, all of them. I grow lots of different greens during the cooler months and pick them young, when they're tender. If you're using more mature greens for this recipe, you can cook them a bit longer. I like my greens to have a really melty texture.

In this recipe, I particularly love the mix of bitterness from the greens, tanginess from the vinegar, and spice from the Frank's Red Hot Sauce, which hails from Louisiana but is now found nationwide. It pairs beautifully with pork, like the braised pork butt in this chapter.

Serves 4

1/4 cup vegetable oil
1/4 cup slivered garlic, plus 1 teaspoon minced garlic
1/4 teaspoon red chile flakes
1/2 pound young collard greens, washed thoroughly and roughly chopped
1/2 pound mustard greens, washed thoroughly and roughly chopped
1/4 cup dry white wine
1 tablespoon red wine vinegar
1 teaspoon sea salt, more to taste
1 teaspoon freshly ground pepper, more to taste
1 teaspoon hot sauce, such as Frank's Red Hot Sauce

In a heavy-bottomed stockpot, heat oil over medium heat and sauté slivered garlic until translucent, about 45 seconds. Add red chile flakes, collards, and mustard greens and sauté until beginning to wilt, about 1 minute. Add wine, 1/4 cup water, and vinegar. Reduce heat to medium-low heat and cook for 20 minutes. Stir in minced garlic. If pot becomes too dry, add more water. (It should look pretty juicy.) Add salt, pepper, and hot sauce. Taste, and adjust seasonings if necessary.

Song: Just Right, Beasts of Bourbon

Song: Highly Inflammable, X-Ray Spex

CURRIED CHICKPEA SALAD

This make-ahead dish is great on its own. It also makes a great filling for a sandwich or green salad topping.

To save leftover canned chipotles, line a metal baking dish with plastic wrap and spread out the chipotles so they do not touch. Freeze, then pluck them off and store in a freezer bag.

Serves 6

2 tablespoons good-quality chutney
1/2 chipotle chile in adobo sauce, minced
1 teaspoon Dijon mustard
1 teaspoon curry powder
1 teaspoon ground cumin
1 tablespoon rice wine vinegar
2 tablespoons vegetable oil
1 teaspoon sea salt, more to taste
1 teaspoon freshly ground pepper, more to taste
1 medium red onion, finely diced
4 cloves garlic, minced
2 cups cooked chickpeas, drained and rinsed if canned
1 cup cooked black beans, drained and rinsed if canned
1/2 cup sun-dried tomatoes in oil, drained and roughly chopped
1/4 cup celery, finely diced
1/4 cup carrots, sliced into 1/2-inch coins
2 tablespoons cilantro, chopped
2 tablespoons parsley, chopped

In a large bowl, whisk together chutney, chipotle, Dijon, curry, cumin, vinegar, oil, salt, and pepper. Mix well (it will be somewhat chunky from the chutney). Add red onion, garlic, chickpeas, black beans, sun-dried tomatoes, celery, carrots, cilantro, and parsley, and fold together with a rubber spatula. Mash the mixture slightly using the back of the spatula (it should be smashed but chunky). Season with salt and pepper to taste and refrigerate for up to 3 days. Serve chilled.

PEAR & CRANBERRY COMPOTE

I love keeping this compote around, especially in fall. It's lovely with yogurt, cottage cheese, toast, ice cream, and many desserts.

Makes 2 pints

3 pounds ripe pears, such as Anjou or Bosc, peeled and diced into 1-inch pieces
2 cups fresh cranberries
1/4 cup freshly squeezed orange juice
1 cup sugar
1 vanilla bean, cut in half and scraped
1/2 teaspoon cinnamon
1/4 teaspoon allspice
1/4 teaspoon freshly grated nutmeg

In a heavy-bottomed, nonreactive pot over high heat, combine pears, cranberries, and orange juice. Bring to a boil, reduce heat to low, and simmer until pears are very soft and cranberries have popped open, about 1 hour.

Remove from heat and mash fruit with a potato masher to consistency of applesauce. Add sugar, vanilla bean, cinnamon, allspice, and nutmeg. Return pot to medium heat and cook the compote until the water from the fruit has mostly evaporated, about 5 minutes. It should be quite thick.

If you want to preserve your compote, follow the directions on page 77. Otherwise, refrigerate in clean, sterilized jars for up to 1 week.

The Auntie Em's Cookbook

Song: Outdoor Miner, Wire

Winter

WINTER

Beet & Blood Orange Salad

Cranberry Beans with Black Kale & Red Chiles

Noah's Vegetarian Breakfast Torta

Best Hot Chocolate

Wilted Spinach & Lentil Salad with Poached Eggs

Baked Eggs in Ham Baskets

Salmon & Fennel Scramble
with Dill Crème Fraîche

Spicy Sausage & Cheddar Grits

Bacon, Onion Sprouts, Avocado & Egg Sandwich

Biscuits & Sausage Gravy

Swiss Chard Gratin

WHAT'S IN SEASON IN WINTER?

Beets

Belgian endive

Broccoli

Broccoli rabe

Brussels sprouts

Cabbage

Cardoons

Cauliflower

Celery

Celery root

Chicory

Clementines

Curly endive
(frisée)

Fennel

Grapefruit

Horseradish

Kale

Kiwis

Kohlrabi

Kumquats

Lemons

Onions

Oranges

Parsnips

Pears

Persimmons

Pommelos

Potatoes

Radicchio

Rutabagas

Satsumas

Shallots

Sunchokes

Sweet potatoes

Tangerines

Treviso

Turnips

Winter squash

NOT-SO-CHILLY SCENES OF WINTER

Winter in L.A.—okay, so it hovers around 70 in the daytime, and it doesn't rain much (but when it does rain, it pours), and everyone complains when it gets to 50 degrees at night. But we still have a season we Angelenos call "winter," and for us at Auntie Em's, it's the busiest time of year. We prepare Thanksgiving pick-up meals for hundreds of people; I swear, no one cooks Thanksgiving dinner anymore. We make hundreds and hundres of pies. At Christmastime, it's cookies and cupcakes and gift baskets. Our catering department is at full crank, with office parties, fancy sit-down dinners, receptions at the mayor's house, fundraisers…you name it, it's happening in December. The whole restaurant works 24-7 during that time, and it's exhausting—but to me, it's also the most fun. Everybody's in the holiday spirit, everybody's in a good mood, and the kitchen and serving crew have a blast being creative together.

And then, as we head deeper into winter in January, we all get a break and a chance to catch up on our sleep. And because it does dip below 60 degrees in the mornings, we serve "warmer" food, as always with a focus on seasonal ingredients, using lots of kale, spinach, chard, beans, citrus, and such. We bring out the hot chocolate, and on really cold mornings, make some biscuits and gravy. You'll find all those recipes in this chapter, to warm up your own winter mornings, which might be a lot colder than mine!

Song: The Witch, The Sonics

BEET & BLOOD ORANGE SALAD

This gorgeous salad is a perfect brunch dish for a crowd. You can prepare everything ahead and assemble it when guests arrive. It's even better the next day, after it has marinated in the dressing.

I love using baby beets—they're a bit tenderer, and I think they're prettier. For a great color combination, I usually use two or three kinds of beets. If you can find them, Chioggia beets are fun; their red and white stripes make them look like candy canes. Add baby Golden and Bull's Blood varieties for a beautiful mix.

Serves 6 as a side salad

6 bunches baby beets, mixed colors, washed and trimmed of their greens

6 cups water

1/2 cup red wine vinegar

1/4 cup sugar

2 tablespoons sea salt, more to taste

3 twists freshly ground pepper, more to taste

Juice of 1 blood orange

1/4 cup apple cider vinegar

1/2 cup extra-virgin olive oil

3 blood oranges, peeled and cut into 1/4-inch-thick disks

1/2 cup basil chiffonade or small leaves

Preheat oven to 400°.

Place beets in a large roasting pan. Add water, red wine vinegar, sugar, salt, and pepper and cover with a lid or foil. Roast until tender when pierced with a knife, about 50 minutes.

Remove lid or foil and set aside beets for 10 minutes, or until cool enough to handle. Wearing thin gloves, slip beets out of their skins. They should slide out easily. Cut into quarters and set aside.

In a medium bowl, whisk together blood orange juice and apple cider vinegar. Slowly drizzle in olive oil while whisking to emulsify. Add salt and pepper to taste. Set aside.

Arrange beets and orange slices on a large platter, drizzle with vinaigrette, and garnish with basil. Season with salt and pepper to taste. Serve immediately.

CRANBERRY BEANS WITH BLACK KALE & RED CHILES

I prefer making my beans from scratch for a dish like this, because canned beans are so mushy. You can find beautiful heirloom beans at specialty stores or online. If you can't find cranberry beans, substitute any small white bean. The bean recipe makes more than you need for this dish, but I like to keep a stash of cooked beans in the fridge.

Feel free to experiment with other greens, such as swiss chard or baby collard greens.

Serves 2 to 3 as a side dish

FOR BEANS:
3/4 cup dried cranberry beans
4 cups water
2 cloves garlic, minced
1 shallot, finely chopped
1 bay leaf
1 dried chile de árbol

Combine beans and water in a medium pot. Bring to a boil, turn off heat, and let soak for 2 hours. Add garlic, shallot, bay leaf, and chile to pot and return to boil. Reduce heat to simmer and cook until beans are tender, about 30 minutes to 1 hour, depending on freshness of beans. Drain water and discard bay leaf. You can refrigerate beans for up to 3 days in water.

FOR KALE:
3 tablespoons extra-virgin olive oil
3 cloves garlic, minced
1/2 onion, diced into 1/2-inch pieces
1 teaspoon fresh rosemary, roughly chopped
1 dried chile de árbol, roughly chopped
2 cups black kale, stemmed and shredded
1 cup water
1 cup cooked cranberry beans, drained
Sea salt and freshly ground pepper

In a large sauté pan, heat oil over medium heat. Add garlic, onion, and rosemary, and cook until onions are translucent, about 1 minute. Add chile, kale, and water and sauté until water is evaporated, about 4 minutes. Add beans and cook another minute or two, until warm. Season with salt and pepper to taste. Serve immediately.

Song: Give Me the Cure, Fugazi

NOAH'S VEGETARIAN BREAKFAST TORTA

I like my black beans pretty creamy, with a few whole beans scattered throughout to give them some contrasting textures. For the chile powder mix, I use a blend of ancho, árbol, and pasilla peppers, but any good chile powder will work. This makes more beans and mole sauce than you'll need, but both can be refrigerated for a few days, and I bet you can find a good use for them!

Makes 6 large sandwiches

FOR BEANS:
3 tablespoons extra-virgin olive oil
1 large onion, finely chopped
6 cloves garlic, minced
1 jalapeño, seeded and minced, or to taste
2 15-ounce cans unseasoned black beans, drained and rinsed,
   or 3 cups homemade beans, drained
1/4 cup water
1 teaspoon ground cumin
1/2 teaspoon ground coriander
2 tablespoons freshly squeezed lemon juice
Sea salt and freshly ground pepper

In a large sauté pan, heat olive oil over medium heat. Add onion and garlic and cook until translucent, 3 to 5 minutes, stirring occasionally. Add jalapeño and cook until tender, about 3 minutes. Add beans and water. Increase heat to medium-high and continue to cook until beans begin to break apart, stirring regularly. Add cumin, coriander, lemon juice, and salt and pepper to taste. Mix well.

Remove beans from heat. For chunkier beans, mash with a potato masher to desired consistency. For smoother beans, pulse in a food processor.

For mole sauce:

1 tablespoon extra-virgin olive oil

1 large onion, diced

4 cloves garlic, minced

1 32-ounce can diced tomatoes

1 cup low-sodium vegetable stock or water

1/4 cup 64% chocolate or semisweet chocolate chips

3 tablespoons chile powder

2 chipotle peppers in adobo sauce (do not rinse), chopped, more adobo sauce to taste

1/4 teaspoon sea salt, more to taste

Freshly ground pepper

In a large sauté pan, heat olive oil over medium heat. Add onion and garlic and cook until translucent, about 3 to 5 minutes, stirring occasionally. Add tomatoes and stock or water, bring to a simmer, and add chocolate, chile powder, chipotles, and salt. Reduce heat to low and simmer for about 15 minutes to allow the flavors to meld, stirring occasionally.

Remove mole from heat. When cool enough to handle, purée in a food processor until smooth. Season with additional salt and pepper to taste. Store extra mole in a tightly sealed jar in the fridge for up to a week.

For tortas:

6 bollilos, teleras, or similar large, soft sandwich roll

1/2 to 3/4 cup Mole Sauce (*see recipe above*)

1 1/2 cups Black Beans (see *recipe previous page*)

6 thin slices sharp cheddar cheese, optional

6 thick tomato slices

3 small avocados, thinly sliced

12 large eggs, scrambled

Lightly toast both sides of bread. Spread top half generously with mole and the bottom half with 4 tablespoons of black beans. Top beans with cheese, if desired. Divide tomato and avocado between sandwiches and top with scrambled eggs. (See scrambled egg instructions on page 190 if needed.) Slice each sandwich in half and serve immediately.

BEST HOT CHOCOLATE

Because this has espresso powder in it, I consider it more of an adult hot chocolate. It is very rich and so, so good.

Makes 4 cups

2 cups whole milk
2 cups half and half
1/2 cup heavy cream
4 ounces 64% chocolate, chopped
4 ounces good-quality milk chocolate, chopped
1 tablespoon sugar
1 teaspoon pure vanilla extract
1 1/2 teaspoons espresso powder

In a medium saucepan, heat milk, half and half, and cream over medium heat until just beginning to simmer. Turn off heat, add both chocolates, and whisk until melted. Add sugar, vanilla extract, and espresso powder and whisk until espresso powder is dissolved. Serve immediately.

Song: Chocolate Jesus, Tom Waits

WILTED SPINACH & LENTIL SALAD WITH POACHED EGGS

By the time winter rolls around on my Eagle Rock farm, my hens' eggs are few and far between—they molt in winter, so they don't lay. And when it's cold, they tend to lay a lot less. So any eggs I can come by are golden. If I don't have any of my own, I head to the farmers' market—freshness counts when poaching eggs.

Serves 4

FOR LENTILS:

1 1/2 cups dried French lentils
2 tablespoons extra-virgin olive oil
1 shallot, minced
3 cloves garlic, minced
1 teaspoon fresh thyme leaves
1 teaspoon flat-leaf parsley, chopped
1 bay leaf
1 teaspoon sea salt
1 teaspoon freshly ground pepper
Enough water to cover lentils
6 cups baby spinach

Rinse lentils and set aside. Place a medium pot over medium heat, add olive oil, and sauté shallots, garlic, thyme, and parsley until shallots and garlic are translucent, about 2 minutes. Add bay leaf, lentils, salt, and pepper and cover beans with 4 inches of water. Bring to a boil over high heat. Turn heat down to medium-low and let simmer gently until lentils are tender, about 25 minutes. Remove from heat, drain lentils, and return them to pot. Add spinach and stir to combine and wilt. Set aside.

Song: Ugly Breakfast, Salamander Jim

FOR DRESSING:

1/4 cup red wine vinegar
1 teaspoon Dijon mustard
1 shallot, minced
1/2 cup extra-virgin olive oil
4 poached eggs

Combine all ingredients in a medium jar. Cover and shake vigorously until emulsified. Add 3 tablespoons of dressing to spinach and lentils, mixing well to coat. Divide salad between 4 plates. Follow the directions on page 191 for poached eggs and top each plate with a poached egg. Serve immediately.

BAKED EGGS IN HAM BASKETS

I came up with these sweet ham baskets for our brunch menu, and they're as delicious as they are pretty. I like to serve them with fresh fruit.

Serves 6

6 thin slices good-quality ham
6 large eggs
6 tablespoons heavy cream, divided
Sea salt and freshly ground pepper
6 sprigs thyme

Preheat oven to 350°.

Spray 6 cups of a muffin pan with nonstick cooking spray. Line each with a slice of ham. Crack an egg into each ham-lined cup and drizzle with 1 tablespoon cream. Sprinkle each with a pinch of salt and pepper, and top with a sprig of thyme. Bake until egg is set but yolk is still runny, about 10 to 15 minutes, depending on the firmness of yolk you prefer.

Ease eggs out of tins with tongs or by hand, and serve immediately.

Song: Winter, The Rolling Stones

SALMON & FENNEL SCRAMBLE WITH DILL CRÈME FRAÎCHE

Although lox is sometimes referred to as smoked salmon, it's actually a different product. Make sure to get a good quality smoked salmon for this dish.

Serves 6

1/4 cup crème fraîche
2 sprigs fresh dill, chopped
1 pinch sea salt
1 or 2 grinds freshly ground pepper
12 large eggs
1/2 cup heavy cream
1 tablespoon extra-virgin olive oil
2 heads fennel, fronds removed and thinly sliced
1/4 pound smoked salmon, diced
Sea salt and freshly ground pepper

In a small mixing bowl, combine crème fraîche, dill, salt, and pepper. Mix well and set aside.

In a large mixing bowl, crack 12 eggs. Add heavy cream and whisk until fully incorporated. Set aside.

In a large sauté pan, heat oil over medium-high heat. When oil is hot, add fennel and sauté until edges begin to brown. Add salmon and stir to combine. Add egg mixture and reduce heat to medium. Cook eggs until they begin to set, then stir with a heatproof spatula so the liquid is now at the bottom of the pan. Repeat until the eggs are cooked through, being careful not to brown eggs. If scrambled eggs are cooking too fast, turn the heat down. Season with salt and pepper to taste.

Divide eggs between 6 plates and top with dill crème fraîche. Serve immediately.

Song: Frying Pan, Captain Beefheart & The Magic Band

SPICY SAUSAGE & CHEDDAR GRITS

These grits are one of our most popular weekend dishes. We serve them topped with two fried eggs, but they're great on their own, too.

Serves 4

6 pork sausage patties
6 cups whole milk
1 teaspoon cayenne pepper
1/2 teaspoon nutmeg
1 teaspoons sea salt
2 teaspoons freshly ground pepper
1 1/2 cups stone-ground white grits
1 tablespoon unsalted butter
1 cup good-quality cheddar cheese

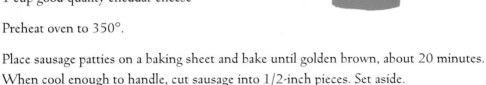

Preheat oven to 350°.

Place sausage patties on a baking sheet and bake until golden brown, about 20 minutes. When cool enough to handle, cut sausage into 1/2-inch pieces. Set aside.

In a large saucepan, combine milk, cayenne, nutmeg, salt, and pepper. Whisk until milk and spices are well combined. Add grits and whisk well. Bring to a boil over high heat, then reduce to medium-low and cook until grits are creamy and smooth, about 20 minutes, stirring occasionally. Remove grits from heat, add butter, and whisk until smooth. Add cheese and sausage and mix well. Serve immediately.

Song: Kielbasa, Tenacious D

BACON, ONION SPROUTS, AVOCADO & EGG SANDWICH

I use onion sprouts for this variation on the BLT. You can find them at your local farmers' market or at quality markets. If you can't find them, substitute alfalfa sprouts.

Makes 2 sandwiches

8 slices thick-cut applewood-smoked bacon
4 slices country white bread, toasted
4 tablespoons mayonnaise
1 cup onion sprouts
1 small avocado, cut into thin slices
1 tablespoon vegetable oil
2 large eggs

In a large, heavy frying pan, cook bacon over medium heat until crispy, about 4 to 5 minutes. Drain on paper towels and set aside.

Spread 1 tablespoon mayonnaise on each slice of toast. Divide onion sprouts between 2 slices and top with avocado and bacon. Set aside.

In a medium nonstick pan, heat oil over medium-high heat. Crack eggs into pan and sauté until the edges are slightly crispy and brown. Flip eggs with a rubber spatula and cook until yolks are set but still runny, about 1 minute. Top each sandwich half with an egg and remaining slice of toast. Serve immediately.

Song: In Heaven, Peter Ivers

Biscuits & Sausage Gravy

Is there any food in the world better than a hot, handmade biscuit? With gravy, or with butter and jam? I've gone to so many diners and ordered a biscuit with the hopes of a flaky, buttery pillow—only to be served a hockey puck. So I made it a mission to make great biscuits, and I really think ours are the best. The secret is making sure your butter and buttermilk are really cold, and that the dough is not over-mixed.

We serve them open faced, topped with sausage gravy, or with a pat of butter and some handmade strawberry vanilla bean jam or marmalade. Heaven!

Makes 12 biscuits & 4 cups gravy

For gravy:
1 pound uncased breakfast sausage
3 tablespoons unsalted butter
1/4 cup flour
2 cups whole milk
1/2 cup heavy cream
1/2 teaspoon sea salt
1 teaspoon freshly ground black pepper

In a small saucepan, brown sausage over medium heat, stirring frequently and breaking up sausage as it cooks. When sausage is no longer pink, add butter and stir to melt. Add flour and mix until no flecks are visible in sausage mixture. Slowly add milk and cream, stirring constantly. Reduce heat to medium-low and add salt and pepper. Cook, stirring often and scraping the bottom of the pan, until gravy has thickened, about 15 minutes. Place gravy in a bain-marie or double boiler to keep warm. Do not leave on stove, as it will break.

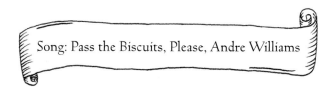

Song: Pass the Biscuits, Please, Andre Williams

For biscuits:

4 cups all-purpose flour	1 teaspoon sugar
4 teaspoons baking powder	1 cup unsalted butter, cold,
1 teaspoon baking soda	cut into 1/2-inch cubes
1 1/2 teaspoons sea salt	2 1/4 cups buttermilk, well chilled, divided

Preheat oven to 375°.

In a large mixing bowl, whisk together flour, baking powder, baking soda, salt, and sugar. Cut butter into flour mixture using a pastry cutter until mixture is crumbly and butter is pea sized. Add 2 cups buttermilk, and mix until just combined.

Turn dough onto a floured surface and knead 3 or 4 times, until just incorporated. Do not over-knead. Pat dough into a circle about 1 1/2 inches thick. Cut biscuits with a 5-inch biscuit cutter. Divide biscuits between 2 baking sheets and brush tops of each with remaining 1/4 cup buttermilk.

Bake until golden brown, 18 to 20 minutes. Allow to cool 5 minutes before topping with gravy and serving.

Song: It's a Rainy Day, Sunshine Girl, Faust

SWISS CHARD GRATIN

Come wintertime, there's something so delish about a vegetable smothered in cheese, butter, and cream. The fresh nutmeg is what really makes this recipe work. You can use rainbow chard, but I don't like the way the red stems bleed into the cream and make it pink, so I stick with the green variety.

Serves 4

1 teaspoon sea salt, more to taste
4 large bunches swiss chard, stems removed but leaves left whole
1/4 cup unsalted butter
1/4 teaspoon flour
3 cloves garlic, minced
1 cup heavy cream
2 1/2 cups whole milk
3 grates fresh nutmeg
1 teaspoon freshly squeezed lemon juice
2 cups freshly grated Parmigiano Reggiano

Preheat oven to 400°.

Bring a large pot of water to a boil. Add salt and chard and boil until tender, about 7 minutes. Drain in a colander and rinse chard under cool water. Place on a clean kitchen towel, squeeze to dry, and dice into 1-inch pieces. Set aside.

In a medium saucepan, heat butter over medium heat. When butter no longer bubbles, whisk in flour. Whisk constantly for about 1 minute, reducing heat if mixture begins to brown. Add garlic, cook for 30 seconds, and then add cream, milk, and nutmeg. Whisk slowly over medium-low heat until sauce thickens, about 4 to 5 minutes.

In a medium casserole dish, layer 1/2 of swiss chard, 1/2 of cream sauce, and 1/2 of cheese. Repeat layers, finishing with cheese. Bake gratin until bubbly and light brown, about 15 to 20 minutes.

DESSERTS & BAKED GOODS

Caramel Monkey Bread

Pecan Sticky Buns

Cinnamon Rolls

Lemony Lemon Bars

Nectarine Hand Pies

Thin & Crispy Chocolate Chip Cookies

Plum Bars

Chocolate Cream Cheese Brownies

Apricot Galette

Oatmeal Cream Pies

Chocolate Pots de Crème with Olive Oil & Sea Salt

Pink Grapefruit Chiffon Cake

Coconut Layer Cake

Green Tea Cake

Nectarine Cornmeal Upside Down Cake

Red Velvet Cupcakes

Caramel Apple Pie

Peach & Pluot Pie

Shaker Lemon Pie

The Baker Who Doesn't Bake

It's no secret that I don't love baking. I am a cook. I can spend hours working to perfect a chicken stock, but somehow I don't have the patience to bake. So I learned early on to hire good bakers. I tell them what I like. We talk, taste, experiment, and taste some more. We keep our desserts simple and made with seasonal ingredients.

At Auntie Em's Kitchen, we always have a seasonal fruit crisp, seasonal bread pudding, and four flavors of cupcakes, as well as layer cakes, puddings, and cookies. I love old-fashioned desserts, so we do a lot of the classics, but we've honed them to suit my tastes. The lemon bars are a bit tangier than most. Our whipped cream is not overly sweet and has real vanilla bean in it. Our pies are more fruity than sugary. And our cupcakes are heaped with enough frosting to have a bite of cake with each taste of frosting. They are very top-heavy. And let me tell you, that was quite a feat to achieve—the cake needs to be sturdy enough to hold all of the frosting, but still be moist.

A lot of people think that butter is the secret to a moist cake, but it's actually vegetable oil. In fact, some years ago the National Dairy Council asked me to be a butter spokesperson, which would have involved flying around the country doing commercials, morning talk shows, and demonstrating recipes with butter. It would have been amazing! But when they found out that our popular cupcakes were made with vegetable oil, they found someone else in a hurry.

CARAMEL MONKEY BREAD

Monkey Bread (so the story goes) first appeared in the 1950s. It also goes by the names of Bubble Bread and Pull-Apart Bread. These muffin-like breads should be served straight out of the oven so they're easy to pull apart. Use the Brioche Dough recipe on page 196.

Makes 12

Preheat oven to 325°.

FOR MONKEY BREAD DOUGH:
Place liners in a 12-count cupcake pan. Set aside.

Take chilled Brioche Dough out of the refrigerator and cut into 3/4-inch slices. Cut each slice into two half-circles and then in half again the other way, creating little 1/2-inch to 1-inch cubes. Fill each cupcake liner about 2/3 full with dough cubes. The dough pieces will settle, so after 5 minutes check amounts and add more cubes as needed. If the dough gets too soft to work with, pop it back in the refrigerator for a couple minutes. Once all tins are filled, lightly cover the pan with plastic wrap and let dough rise in a warm area until it has risen to fill cupcake pans and is very light to the touch, 45 minutes to 1 hour. Remove plastic wrap and bake until tops are golden brown and edges are springy to the touch, 15 to 20 minutes. The centers will still be soft. Remove from the oven and let cool in the pan for 5 to 10 minutes.

VARIATION: If you want a sweeter monkey bread, combine 1/4 cup brown sugar, 1/4 cup white sugar, and 1 1/2 teaspoons cinnamon. Sprinkle over chopped dough pieces before placing them in the cupcake tins.

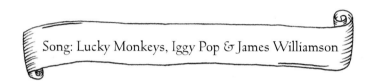

Song: Lucky Monkeys, Iggy Pop & James Williamson

FOR CARAMEL SAUCE:

3/4 cup granulated sugar

1 tablespoon corn syrup

5 tablespoons water

2 tablespoons unsalted butter,
   at room temperature

1/3 cup heavy cream

1/4 teaspoon kosher salt

Combine sugar, corn syrup, and water in a small pot. Use a damp pastry brush to wipe down any sugar crystals stuck to sides of the pot. Place the pot over medium-high heat. Do not stir. If the sugar mixture is boiling or coloring unevenly, gently swirl the pot. When the sugar mixture begins to brown, keep a close eye on it, and when it reaches a deep golden brown, remove the pot from the heat. Briskly whisk the butter, cream, and salt into the sugar. Wear an oven mitt or use a long-handled whisk, as the caramel will bubble and produce a large cloud of steam. Set aside to cool.

Take monkey bread out of the pan and drizzle with warm caramel. Enjoy!

Pecan Sticky Buns

We make these only on the weekends at Auntie Em's, because they're a bit labor intensive. And it's a good thing that we don't make them more often, because it kills me when we have them out. It's the combination of the pillowy-soft, warm dough, buttery caramel, and crunchy pecans—I seriously have to stay away or I will eat the whole damn thing. These are lovely to make when you're having special guests. Serve them with a pot of drip coffee and warmed milk.

1/4 cup granulated sugar

1/4 cup brown sugar

1 teaspoon salt

1/2 cup unsalted butter, at room temperature

1/2 cup corn syrup

1/2 teaspoon vanilla extract

2 cups whole pecans, roughly chopped

1 Brioche Dough (*see recipe page 196*)

Song: Sticky and Sweet, Cows

Using a stand mixer fitted with the paddle attachment, cream both sugars, salt, and butter on high speed until fluffy and pale in color, about 5 minutes. Add corn syrup and vanilla and mix on medium-high until light and airy, about 3 minutes. Divide sugar mixture in half. Save one half for another day. It can be refrigerated for up to a month or frozen for up to 3 months.

Use a small offset spatula or the back of a spoon to evenly spread the remaining half of the sugar mixture base over the bottom of a 9-inch cake pan. Sprinkle pecan pieces over prepared pan. Gently press nuts into the sticky base.

Pull out brioche dough from refrigerator. Cut into 6 equal pieces, each about 1 1/2 inches wide. Place one piece in the center of cake pan and arrange the other five pieces around it in a circle. Cover lightly with plastic wrap and let rest in a warm area until dough rises to cover gaps between the buns and is very soft to the touch, 1 to 1 1/2 hours.

Preheat oven to 350°.

Uncover and bake until tops are golden brown and edges are springy to the touch, about 1 hour. Wait at least 30 minutes before opening oven door to check on bread, and check quickly. The buns will sink in the middle if the oven is left open for too long while baking.

Remove buns from oven and let cool for 10 to 15 minutes. Gently run a sharp knife around edge of the pan and place a serving plate upside down on top of buns. Carefully flip buns and serving plate upside down, and slowly remove the cake pan. If the pan does not easily come off when flipped, the sticky bottom has cooled too much. You can gently reheat the bottom of pan over a burner on the stove or with a kitchen blowtorch for 30 seconds to 1 minute. Be careful, though, as you only want to warm the caramel, not burn the buns, and the metal pan will get hot very quickly.

CINNAMON ROLLS

When touring, it's sometimes really hard to find good food—you just see fast-food place after fast-food place. So when we'd head up Interstate 5 to tour the west coast, we were always happy to stop at a little trucker café between Medford and Eugene in Oregon called Heaven on Earth. It was (and still is) known for its "family-sized" cinnamon rolls, which we called "size of your head" cinnamon rolls. We always stopped for a meal and then each took a cinnamon roll for the road. I remember one morning when it was my turn to drive, leaving Heaven on Earth and watching the sun come up as we headed to our next venue. I nibbled on that giant cinnamon roll for hours. I can still picture it sitting up there on the dashboard in our beat-up old van. Huge and beautiful.

Our cinnamon rolls at Auntie Em's aren't quite that big, but they're just as delicious. They are best enjoyed warm.

1 Brioche Dough (*see recipe page 196*)
1 1/4 cups powdered sugar
1/4 teaspoon vanilla extract
2 tablespoons whole milk, heated, more as needed

Take chilled dough out of the refrigerator and cut into 6 pieces, about 1 1/2 inches thick. Place one piece in the center of an unlined 9-inch cake pan, and arrange the other five pieces in a circle around it. Lightly cover with plastic wrap and set in a warm area to rise until dough fills gaps between rolls and is very soft to the touch, 1 to 1 1/2 hours.

Preheat oven to 350°.

Remove plastic wrap and bake for 45 minutes to 1 hour. Rotate pan after 30 minutes, but work quickly as the buns will sink if the oven is open for too long. Buns are done when tops are evenly browned and edges are springy to the touch. If the center bun sinks, in the future keep oven closed longer or add five minutes to the baking time. Let buns cool at least 15 to 20 minutes, until warm but not hot to the touch.

Sift powdered sugar into a medium bowl. Add vanilla and hot milk and whisk quickly until smooth. If glaze is too thick, add additional milk 1 teaspoon at a time until it reaches desired consistency. If it is too thin, add more powdered sugar 2 tablespoons at a time. Glaze will thicken as it cools.

Once buns are cool, gently run a sharp knife around edge of the pan and place a plate upside down on top of buns. Carefully flip buns and serving plate upside down, and slowly remove the cake pan. Place a serving plate on bottom of the buns and flip back over. Use a spoon to drizzle buns with glaze. If the buns have completely cooled, reheat before glazing.

For variations, try adding 1/2 teaspoon of cinnamon or cocoa powder to the powdered sugar when making the glaze.

Song: Baby Lemonade, Syd Barrett

LEMONY LEMON BARS

These lemon bars are totally old school. Just the thought of them makes my mouth water. Pick up juicy, ripe lemons at the farmers' market during the winter for the best results, and choose regular lemons rather than Meyers—you want the tartness. The crust recipe requires pie weights, or you can line the bottom of the crust with parchment or foil and cover with a layer of dried beans.

Makes 24 bars

FOR THE CRUST:
8 ounces unsalted butter, chilled, cut into 1-inch pieces
1 2/3 cups flour
2/3 cup powdered sugar

Place butter, flour, and sugar in bowl of a stand mixer fitted with the paddle attachment and mix on medium-low speed until dough comes together in a rough ball, about 2 minutes. Form dough into a rectangle about 1/2-inch thick, cover with plastic wrap, and refrigerate until firm enough to roll out, about 30 minutes. Spray a 9″ × 13″ baking pan with nonstick cooking spray or rub with butter. Line pan with enough parchment paper, width-wise, so 1-inch of paper hangs over edges. Roll dough into an 11″ × 15″ rectangle and gently place in pan so dough goes up sides of pan. Use dough scraps to patch any holes. Refrigerate 30 minutes.

Preheat oven to 350° and place rack in middle of oven.

Remove pan from refrigerator and line bottom with parchment paper and pie weights. The bottom should be completely covered with pie weights. Bake until edges of crust just begin to brown, about 16 to 18 minutes, rotating pan after 10 minutes. Remove pie weights and bake until bottom of crust just begins to brown, about 10 to 12 minutes more. Set aside to cool.

FOR THE FILLING:

2 2/3 cups granulated sugar

Zest of 3 large lemons (about 1 tablespoon, packed)

Juice of 4 large lemons (about 1/2 cup plus 2 tablespoons)

6 large eggs

3 1/2 tablespoons flour

1/2 teaspoon baking powder

In a large bowl, whisk together sugar, zest, lemon juice, and eggs until combined.

Sift together flour and baking powder and add to wet ingredients. Whisk vigorously until no lumps remain. Place baked crust on oven rack and pour in filling. Bake until crust is brown and filling is set but not hard to the touch, 40 to 45 minutes, rotating pan after 25 minutes. If edges of crust begin to look too dark after 25 minutes, cover edges only loosely with foil. Let cool 1 hour before slicing into bars.

NECTARINE HAND PIES

These little pies fit in your hand, making them perfect for a picnic or travel. Make sure to taste the nectarines before buying them (or at least before making the pies) to make sure they're sweet and delicious.

HINT:

Roll out the dough first, then refrigerate it. It needs to chill for about the amount of time it takes to prepare the filling. This recipe will also be a little easier if you've made ravioli before, because the technique is similar.

Song: Dyna-mite, Mud

Makes 6 hand pies

1 Cream Cheese Pie Dough (*see recipe page 194*)
4 tablespoons unsalted butter, melted
1 1/4 cups nectarines (about 3), diced into 1/2-inch to 3/4-inch cubes, peeled if you prefer
2 tablespoons orange juice
1 tablespoon cornstarch for juicy fruit, 2 teaspoons for drier fruit
3 tablespoons granulated sugar
1 egg
1 1/2 tablespoons water
Raw sugar, for sprinkling

Roll out pie dough into a 6″ × 24″ rectangle, cut in half, and place on two large baking sheets. Brush top of dough with melted butter. Refrigerate for 15 to 20 minutes.

Preheat the oven to 375°.

Place chopped nectarines, orange juice, cornstarch, and sugar in a medium bowl. Toss together, either by hand or with a rubber spatula, until fruit is evenly coated.

Pull out prepared dough. Make 3 evenly spaced piles of fruit lengthwise along the center of each dough rectangle. Each pile should have about 3 heaping tablespoons of fruit and be spaced 1 1/2 inch to 2 inches apart. Mix egg with water in a small bowl and brush on the crust between fruit, as well as the top and bottom edges. Take bottom edge of the dough and fold it up to the top, so fruit is at the bottom of a long pocket. Starting in the middle, gently pat dough down around each little pile of fruit. Try to squeeze out any excess air. Use a rolling pastry cutter or pizza cutter to slice pies apart. Take a fork and squish the edges of each pie together, trying not to poke holes in the crust covering the fruit. Use the pastry or pizza cutter to trim the crust down to about 1 to 1 1/2 inch. Each little pie should be about 3 × 3 1/2 to 4 inches.

Brush tops with egg mixture and sprinkle with raw sugar (granulated sugar can be substituted). Cut 3 little slits in the top of each pie. Bake until crusts are a deep golden brown and any visible juices bubble, about 40 to 50 minutes. Let cool for 5 to 10 minutes and enjoy!

THIN & CRISPY CHOCOLATE CHIP COOKIES

These thin, chewy chocolate-y disks were featured on *Sugar High* on the Food Network. The host, Duff Goldman, came to Auntie Em's, and I demonstrated the recipe for him. We had a really fun time together. We did a shot where we rode his motorcycle to my house to get eggs from my chickens. I talked the producers into it because I wanted my chickens on TV!

The bakers at Auntie Em's worked on this recipe for months and months, because I knew exactly what I wanted, but it was not easy to figure it out. One key note: Do not skip the freezer part. The batter is thin, and freezing helps keep it from becoming one giant cookie as opposed to six large cookies. One other tip: Use bars of chocolate chopped into chunks instead of chocolate chips, because it gives the cookies a nice rustic look.

Makes 40 cookies

1 cup unsalted butter, at room temperature

1 cup granulated sugar

1 cup brown sugar

2 large eggs

3 tablespoons water

1 tablespoon plus 1 teaspoon vanilla

1 1/3 cups flour

1/2 teaspoon baking soda

3/4 teaspoon sea salt

1 1/2 cups chopped semisweet baking bar or 64% chocolate pistoles

Song: Blues for My Cookie, Lightnin' Hopkins

Using a stand mixer fitted with the paddle attachment, cream butter and sugars together until light and fluffy, about 4 minutes, scraping down sides of bowl with a rubber spatula occasionally. Reduce to low speed and add eggs one at a time, scraping down the bowl between each. Pour in water and vanilla and mix well.

Mix flour, baking soda, and salt in a medium bowl and add to butter mixture. Mix until incorporated. Fold in chocolate pieces.

Scoop heaped tablespoons of cookie batter on a sheet tray, side by side, and freeze 1 hour, or refrigerate 2 to 3 hours.

Preheat oven to 350°.

Place chilled cookie dough on a parchment-lined baking sheet about 5 inches apart, no more than 6 cookies per tray. Gently press tops of cookies to slightly flatten into discs. Bake 12 to 16 minutes, rotating halfway through. Cookies are done when center is golden brown and edges are set. Let cool on baking sheet for 15 to 20 min, as they crisp while they cool.

Extra batter can be frozen.

Song: Looking For a Kiss, New York Dolls

PLUM BARS

I'm a fruit dessert girl rather than a chocolate dessert girl, and this is one of my absolute favorites. The cake is slightly sweet, and the plums add a great tanginess. Try them with the Pear & Cranberry Compote found on page 116—that's what we did for the photograph here.

1/2 cup unsalted butter, at room temperature
1 1/4 cup granulated sugar
1 large egg, plus 1 yolk
1 1/4 teaspoon vanilla extract
1 3/4 cups plus 2 tablespoons flour
1 3/4 teaspoons baking powder
1/2 teaspoon sea salt
2/3 cup milk
3 ripe plums

Preheat oven to 325°. Spray or butter and flour an 9″ × 13″ baking pan. Set aside.

Using a stand mixer fitted with the paddle attachment, cream butter and sugar on high speed until light and fluffy. Scrape down sides of bowl with a rubber spatula and reduce speed to medium. Add eggs and vanilla and mix until fully incorporated.

In a medium bowl, whisk together flour, baking powder, and salt. Add half the flour mixture to butter mixture on low speed, until just incorporated, and pour in milk while mixer is running. Scrape down sides of bowl and add remaining flour. Mix well, scraping down sides of bowl as needed, until batter is smooth. Pour batter into prepared baking pan.

Cut plums into 1/4-inch thick slices and arrange in rows, or another design of your choosing, on top of batter. Bake until cake is golden brown and somewhat springy to the touch, about 45 to 50 minutes. A toothpick inserted into the center should come out clean.

Let cool for at least 10 minutes before slicing.

CHOCOLATE CREAM CHEESE BROWNIES

These delightful treats are more cakey than dense, and thus a bit lighter than a traditional brownie.

Makes 9 large brownies

FOR CHEESECAKE SWIRL:

8 ounces cream cheese, at room temperature

3 tablespoons sugar

1 large egg, at room temperature

1/2 teaspoon vanilla extract

In a stand mixer fitted with the paddle attachment, blend cream cheese and sugar until creamy, about 1 minute. Scrape down sides of bowl with a rubber spatula and add egg. Mix until smooth. Scrape bowl down again and add vanilla. Mix until smooth. Cover and refrigerate for 1 hour, so cream cheese mixture will set and thicken.

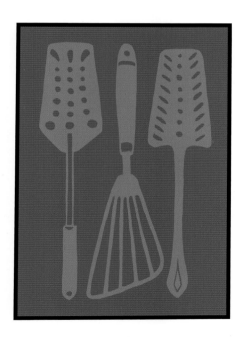

Song: Higher Ground, Red Hot Chili Peppers

FOR BROWNIE BASE:

1/2 cup unsalted butter, cut into 1-inch pieces

4 ounces 64% chocolate or semisweet chocolate, chopped into 1-inch pieces

2 cups granulated sugar

4 large eggs

1 teaspoon vanilla extract

1 1/2 cups flour

Preheat oven to 350°.

Melt butter in a heavy saucepan over low heat, stirring occasionally. Add chocolate and stir gently until melted. Remove from heat and set aside to cool.

In a medium bowl, whisk together sugar, eggs, and vanilla until thoroughly combined. Slowly mix in the warm (not hot!) melted chocolate mixture and whisk until smooth. Fold in flour with a rubber spatula until blended.

Spray a 9″ × 9″ baking dish with nonstick cooking spray and flour lightly. Pour brownie base into prepared baking dish. Spoon cheesecake filling on top in 6 to 8 separate spoonfuls. Use a butter knife to swirl the cheesecake into the brownies. Swirl more for a creamy brownie, less for a brownie with cheesecake bites. Bake for 50 to 60 minutes, rotating pan halfway through. Brownies are done when a toothpick comes out with a few crumbs and the top is springy to the touch. Let cool for 1 hour, or just dig right in when they are hot, like I do!

APRICOT GALETTE

Apricots are one of my favorite fruits to bake with. When their tanginess is paired with the brown sugar in the recipe, the result is out of this world.

1 Cream Cheese Pie Dough (*see recipe page 194*)
3 tablespoons unsalted butter, melted
1 1/2 pounds apricots
1/2 cup brown sugar
2 tablespoons cornstarch
3 tablespoons orange juice
1 large egg, beaten
3 tablespoons honey, warmed
Raw or turbinado sugar, for sprinkling, if desired

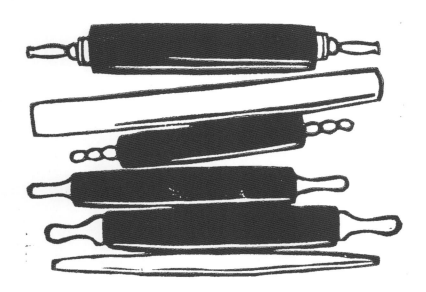

On a lightly floured work surface, roll out pie dough into a 12-inch circle. Place on a flat baking sheet. Brush the center with melted butter, leaving a 1-inch border around the edges. Refrigerate for at least 30 minutes while making the filling.

Cut apricots into 3/4-inch slices. In a medium bowl, combine apricots, brown sugar, cornstarch, and orange juice. Toss to evenly coat apricots.

Pile apricots into center of the pie shell, leaving a 2- to 3-inch border of pie dough. Gently fold one side of pie dough partially over the fruit, and brush the outside with beaten egg. Turn the galette 1/4 turn, fold up the next side, brush with egg, and repeat until all sides are folded and the entire crust has been brushed with egg. The folded dough will not meet in the center; some fruit will be exposed. Be very gentle while folding the dough—if it breaks, the filling will seep out. Patch any holes by trimming a small piece of dough from an edge where it will go unnoticed, brush the area with egg, and gently press on the patch. If a crunchy crust is desired, sprinkle galette with raw or turbinado sugar. Refrigerate 15 minutes.

Preheat oven to 375°.

Bake until crust is an even brown and fruit filling begins to bubble, about 1 hour. Cool until filling begins to set for 10 to 15 minutes. Brush exposed fruit with warmed honey. Serve.

Song: The Wild One, Suzi Quatro

Tips:
Do not skip either refrigeration step. The dough needs time to rest or it will shrink during baking. Also, you can warm the honey by popping it in the microwave for 10 seconds.

OATMEAL CREAM PIES

Remember Little Debbie Oatmeal Cream Pies? This is the Auntie Em's take on them, but we use a cream cheese filling instead. They're great to bring to a potluck or picnic.

Makes 16 cream pies

FOR COOKIES:

1 cup unsalted butter, at room temperature
3/4 cup brown sugar
1/2 cup granulated sugar
1 tablespoon molasses
2 large eggs
1 teaspoon vanilla extract
1 3/4 cups flour
1/2 teaspoon sea salt
1 teaspoon baking soda
1/4 teaspoon cinnamon
1 1/2 cups rolled oats (not quick-cooking)

Song: Blockbuster, Sweet

Using a stand mixer fitted with the paddle attachment, cream butter, both sugars, and molasses until mixture becomes fluffy and light in color. Add eggs one at a time, scraping down bowl halfway through with a spatula. Add vanilla and mix well.

In a medium bowl, combine flour, salt, baking soda, and cinnamon. Add dry ingredients to wet mixture until just blended. Stir in oats.

Scoop dough onto a cookie sheet in heaping tablespoons. Chill for 1 hour.

Preheat oven to 325°.

Shape chilled cookies into balls and return to lined baking sheets 2 inches apart, about 8 per baking sheet. Slightly flatten cookies to a 3/4-inch thickness. Bake for 15 minutes, rotating halfway through. Cookies will be golden brown. Let cool on baking sheet.

For filling:

1/2 cup unsalted butter, at room temperature
6 ounces cream cheese, at room temperature
1/2 teaspoon vanilla extract
1 3/4 cups powdered sugar, sifted

Using a stand mixer fitted with the paddle attachment, cream butter until smooth. Add cream cheese and vanilla and mix until evenly combined and free of lumps. Add powdered sugar and mix until smooth and creamy, scraping down sides of bowl with a rubber spatula a couple of times.

To assemble cream pie:

Flip over half of oatmeal cookies and scoop 1 heaping tablespoon of frosting onto the bottom of each. Top with another cookie and gently press together, making a sandwich. Cream pies will keep up to 4 days in the refrigerator if wrapped in plastic or stored in an airtight container. Place parchment paper between layers of cream pies as they will stick together if they touch.

CHOCOLATE POTS DE CRÈME WITH OLIVE OIL & SEA SALT

I first made this dessert for a dinner party at my house, and my friend Sharon flipped out. So I started making it more often. It has that perfect combination of salty, creamy, and sweet. The recipe calls for you to drizzle the top with sea salt and olive oil, and I also serve extra of each at the table, because I want them with every bite!

Song: Chocolate River, The Seeds

Makes 6 individual pots

1 1/2 cups whole milk
1/2 cup heavy cream
1/4 cup plus 1 tablespoon granulated sugar
1 vanilla bean, split and scraped out
1 cup 64% or semisweet chocolate, roughly chopped
5 large egg yolks
Good quality extra-virgin olive oil to taste
Coarse sea salt

Preheat oven to 300°.

In a heavy-bottomed pot, combine milk, cream, sugar, and vanilla bean seeds and pod. Cook over medium heat until boiling and sugar is dissolved. Remove from heat and add chocolate pieces. Let cool for 3 minutes, and then whisk until chocolate pieces are all melted and mixture is smooth. Set aside.

Whisk egg yolks in a medium bowl until lightened in color. While whisking, slowly add warm chocolate mixture and mix until fully incorporated. It is helpful to have a kitchen assistant for this step because the egg yolks can become scrambled eggs if the chocolate mixture is too hot or added too quickly.

Strain to remove vanilla bean pod and any unmelted chocolate or cooked egg yolk. Divide mixture between 6 4-ounce oven-safe ramekins. Place the ramekins in a large roasting pan or a baking pan with at least a 2-inch edge. Fill roasting pan with enough hot water so it comes halfway up the sides of the ramekins. Carefully put the entire roasting or baking pan, with water and ramekins, in the oven and bake for about 1 hour. The puddings should be relatively set, but will still wiggle slightly in the center when shaken. Remove and let cool in the water bath for a half hour before removing ramekins. The ramekins should then be chilled for 2 to 4 hours, until cold and fully set.

To serve, give each pot de crème a drizzle of your favorite olive oil and a sprinkle of sea salt.

PINK GRAPEFRUIT CHIFFON CAKE

This angel food cake uses a tiny bit of pink food coloring, which you can leave out, but I think the very light pink makes it so cute! If you're not a grapefruit fan, you can substitute any other citrus fruit.

Makes 1 10-inch cake

2 1/4 cups flour
1/2 teaspoon salt
1 tablespoon baking powder
1 1/2 cups granulated sugar, divided
7 large egg yolks
1/2 cup vegetable oil

3/4 cup grapefruit juice
3 tablespoons grapefruit zest
2 teaspoons vanilla extract
9 large egg whites
1 teaspoon cream of tartar

Preheat oven to 325°.

Sift flour, salt, baking powder, and 3/4 cup sugar into a large bowl. In a separate bowl, whisk together egg yolks, oil, juice, zest, and vanilla extract. Combine flour and egg yolk mixtures and mix well. Set aside.

Using a stand mixer fitted with the whisk attachment, beat egg whites and cream of tartar on medium speed until frothy. With mixer running, add remaining sugar one tablespoon at a time. When all the sugar has been added, increase speed to high and whip egg whites until they hold medium peaks.

Mix 1/4 of the whipped egg whites into yolk-flour mixture to soften the batter. Very gently fold in the remaining egg whites in 3 additions. It is very important not to overmix the batter as it will lose the fluffiness the egg whites create.

Pour batter into a 10-inch tube pan or angel food cake pan. It is very important not to spray or butter the tube pan, as the cake climbs the sides as it bakes.

Song: Pink Pussycat, Devo

Bake until a toothpick come out with a few crumbs, 45 minutes to 1 hour. Flip cake upside down to cool. Unless you have a tube pan with built-in feet, you will need to place something under the center to lift the pan a little, otherwise the cake will stick to the table or cooling rack. A small ramekin flipped upside down works nicely. Let cool completely, 30 to 45 minutes.

FOR GRAPEFRUIT SYRUP:

3/4 cup freshly squeezed grapefruit juice

1 cup sugar

Combine juice and sugar in a small pot. Cook over medium heat, swirling gently when the edges begin to bubble. When entire mixture begins to boil, remove from heat. Set aside to cool.

FOR WHIPPED CREAM FROSTING:

3 cups heavy whipping cream

1/4 cup powdered sugar

1 teaspoon vanilla extract

1 to 2 drops pink food coloring

Using a stand mixer fitted with the whisk attachment, combine cream, powdered sugar, and vanilla. Mix on medium or high speed until fully combined. Add food coloring to create desired color. A little goes a long way. Continue to mix until whipped cream just holds its shape. If you overmix, add more cream 2 tablespoons at a time until whipped cream reaches the proper consistency. Refrigerate.

ASSEMBLING THE CAKE:

When the cake is cool, gently run a paring knife around the outer and inner edges of the cake. Flip cake onto a platter or cake board. Pour the grapefruit syrup over top of cake 1/4 cup at a time, trying not to spill it over the edges. If syrup is not being absorbed, use a fork or skewer to gently poke holes in the top of cake. As syrup soaks in, add the rest, 1/4 cup at a time, until the cake is thoroughly soaked. Let all syrup absorb before moving on to the next step.

Use the whipped cream frosting to cover the top, sides, and center of the cake. If desired, use a piping bag and a star frosting tip to decorate top of the cake with rosettes.

COCONUT LAYER CAKE

This coconut cake epitomizes winter to me. It looks like a big snowball, it's really rich in flavor, and the touch of almond extract gives it an extra layer of complexity.

When we were doing the photo shoot for this book, I snuck off with the cake and piled it high with my collection of vintage ceramic and glass dogs. When I reappeared with it, everyone on the shoot burst out laughing. I love to treat desserts as playful pieces of art and decorate them with a lot of whimsy, and I encourage you to do the same.

This coconut cake is the basis for a lot of our wedding cakes. And of all the cakes we make, I really think this one is the most beautiful.

Makes 1 8-inch layer cake

2 1/2 cups flour	2 eggs
1 teaspoon baking soda	1 teaspoon vanilla extract
1 teaspoon salt	1 teaspoon almond extract
1 cup plus 3 tablespoons vegetable oil	1 cup buttermilk
1 1/2 cups granulated sugar	1/2 cup sweetened shredded coconut

Preheat oven to 325°. Spray and line 2 8-inch cake pans. Set aside.

In a medium bowl, combine flour, baking soda, and salt. Whisk to combine and set aside.

Using a stand mixer fitted with the paddle attachment, combine vegetable oil, sugar, eggs, and extracts on low speed. Once ingredients are slightly mixed, increase speed to medium and mix until well combined. Turn speed down to low and add half the flour mixture. Mix until just combined, and then scrape down sides of bowl with a rubber spatula. With mixer running on low speed, slowly add buttermilk until incorporated. Scrape down sides of bowl and add remaining flour. Mix until smooth, scraping down sides of bowl as needed. Add shredded coconut and mix until it is evenly distributed throughout the batter. Divide batter evenly between prepared cake pans. Bake until tops of cakes begin to brown and are springy to the touch, about 40 minutes.

Let cakes cool in the pans until cool to the touch, about 30 minutes.

The Auntie Em's Cookbook

CREAM CHEESE FROSTING

3 cups powdered sugar
3/4 cup butter, softened
1 teaspoon vanilla extract
10 ounces (about 1 1/2 packages) cream cheese, softened

Sift powdered sugar into a medium bowl and set aside.

Using a stand mixer fitted with the paddle attachment, beat the butter and vanilla on medium speed until creamy. Add cream cheese and mix on medium-low until smooth but not airy. Turn the mixer to low and add the powdered sugar one cup at a time. Scrape down the sides of the bowl with a rubber spatula between cups of sugar. Mix on low until smooth and creamy, but not fluffy. If the finished frosting is very soft, refrigerate until firm, 20 to 30 minutes.

ASSEMBLING CAKE:

About 2 cups sweetened shredded coconut, unsweetened if you prefer.

Set one piece of cake on a cake board or platter. Scoop about 2 cups of frosting on cake and use an offset frosting spatula to smooth frosting to edges. Add more frosting if needed to create a 1/2-inch to 3/4-inch layer of frosting. Place second cake upside down on frosting. This gives the cake a nice flat top. Refrigerate 15 to 30 minutes to let frosting firm up. Remove cake from refrigerator and use remaining frosting to coat top and sides of the cake. Pat shredded coconut onto the sides and top of the cake. Enjoy!

Song: The Coconut, Thee Oh Sees

Coconut Layer Cake

Green Tea Cake

GREEN TEA CAKE

Auntie Em's is five minutes from L.A.'s Chinatown, which was the inspiration for this delicious pale green cake. For a stunning presentation, decorate it with light green succulents.

You can find matcha green tea powder at specialty Asian food markets and online.

Makes 1 8-inch layer cake

2 cups flour
3/4 teaspoon sea salt
1 teaspoon baking soda
1 tablespoon matcha green tea powder
1 1/4 cups granulated sugar
2 large eggs

1 cup vegetable oil
1 teaspoon vanilla extract
2 teaspoons water
1 cup buttermilk, divided

Green Tea Cream Cheese Frosting
(*see recipe next page*)

Preheat oven to 325°. Grease (spray or butter) 2 8-inch round cake pans and line with cake liners or cut-out circles of parchment paper. Grease top of the liner as well. Set aside.

In a medium bowl, stir together flour, salt, baking soda, and green tea powder. Set aside.

In a large bowl, whisk together sugar, eggs, oil, vanilla, and water. Mix until ingredients are fully combined and mixture is a uniform yellow. Using a rubber spatula, fold in half the flour mixture. Add buttermilk 1/2 cup at a time and mix well. Mix in remaining flour mixture and whisk to remove any lumps. Divide batter evenly between the prepared cake pans. Bake until the cake is springy to the touch and a toothpick inserted into the center comes out clean, about 30 to 40 minutes. Set aside to cool.

Set 1 cake on a cake board or platter. Scoop about 2 cups frosting onto the cake and use an offset spatula to smooth frosting to the edges. Add more if needed to create a 1/2-inch to 3/4-inch layer of frosting. Place second cake upside down on frosting. This gives the cake a nice flat top. Refrigerate for 15 to 30 minutes to let frosting firm up. Remove cake from refrigerator and use remaining frosting to coat top and sides of the cake.

GREEN TEA CREAM CHEESE FROSTING

Makes about 5 cups

3 cups powdered sugar
1 tablespoon matcha green tea powder
3/4 cup unsalted butter, softened
1 teaspoon vanilla extract
10 ounces cream cheese, softened
3 drops green food coloring (optional)

Sift together powdered sugar and green tea powder in a medium bowl and set aside.

Using a stand mixer fitted with the paddle attachment, beat butter and vanilla on medium speed until creamy. Add cream cheese and mix on medium-low until smooth, but no longer (you don't want it to start adding volume). Turn mixer to low and add powdered sugar mixture 1 cup at a time. Scrape down the sides of the bowl with a rubber spatula between each addition. Mix on low until smooth but not fluffy. If using green food coloring, add one drop at a time until frosting reaches desired color. If the frosting is very soft, refrigerate until firm, about 20 to 30 minutes.

Song: Green Fuz, The Cramps

NECTARINE CORNMEAL UPSIDE DOWN CAKE

My friend Annika, who created all the woodcuts and drawings in the book, says this cake is her very favorite. She has it on her birthday instead of a traditional layer cake. It's not too sweet, and if you don't have nectarines, you can use any stone fruit; we do it quite often with plums.

FOR CARAMEL TOPPING:

Song: Gudbuy T' Jane, Slade

3/4 cup unsalted butter
3/4 cup plus 2 1/2 tablespoons brown sugar

In a heavy bottomed saucepan, melt butter over medium heat. Whisk in brown sugar, reduce heat to low, and cook, stirring constantly, until mixture is smooth and caramel-colored. Pour into an unlined, ungreased, 8-inch cake pan. Set aside to cool. If the kitchen is too warm for the caramel to set, refrigerate for 10 to 15 minutes, until caramel has firmed up but not hardened.

FOR CAKE:

3/4 cup unsalted butter, at room
    temperature
3/4 cup granulated sugar
1 cup flour
1/4 cup cornmeal

1 1/2 teaspoons baking powder
3/4 teaspoon sea salt
3 large eggs plus 1 yolk
1 1/2 teaspoons vanilla extract
4 medium nectarines

Using a stand mixer fitted with the paddle attachment, cream butter and sugar on medium-high speed until very pale and fluffy, about 6 to 8 minutes. While butter and sugar are creaming, mix flour, cornmeal, baking powder, and salt together in a medium bowl and set aside. When butter is well mixed, reduce speed to medium and add eggs and yolk one at a time. Scrape down the bowl between each addition, and be sure each egg is fully incorporated before adding another. This step is important as it helps keep the cake light.

Once all eggs are mixed in, add the vanilla. Reduce mixer to low and add flour-cornmeal mixture. Scrape down sides and bottom of the bowl with a rubber spatula and mix one more minute, until batter is smooth and pale yellow. Set aside.

The Auntie Em's Cookbook

Preheat oven to 325°.

Slice nectarines into 1/4-inch to 1/2-inch slices. Arrange slices on top of caramel-lined cake pan in a pretty design of your choosing. A flower or pinwheel design is simple to do and always looks great. Pour cake batter over the fruit/caramel base and spread to evenly cover the fruit. Bake until top just begins to turn golden and a toothpick inserted into center comes out clean, 50 minutes to 1 hour. Let cool in pan for 10 to 15 minutes. Place cake plate on top of pan and use oven mitts to carefully invert the cake onto the plate. Gently slide pan up and off to reveal your beautiful cake!

Tips:

If any fruit falls off the cake once it's been plated, use a toothpick to hold it back in place until the cake cools. Once it cools, the sticky caramel topping will hold the fruit in place.

If the cake cools for more than 15 minutes, the caramel topping will cool too much and the cake will not come out of the pan. If this happens, gently reheat the bottom of the pan on a stove burner, using low heat, before trying to plate the cake. Another option is to flip the cake, but before pulling off the pan, heat the bottom of the pan with a kitchen blowtorch. With either method, use oven mitts! You are reheating both a metal pan and the caramel inside it, so exercise caution.

RED VELVET CUPCAKES

One day, fairly early on in Auntie Em's history, the producers from *Throwdown with Bobby Flay* invited me to do a segment, and I made red velvet cupcakes. It was such a blast, even though I lost the throwdown. But what came after it aired was insane—business tripled, literally overnight. It was amazing but completely overwhelming. There was a line around the block to get cupcakes—no one seemed to care that I'd lost! People actually flew in from other states to take a picture with me and have a cupcake. It was so crazy that the staff and I had to really rework how we were running the restaurant. We figured it out, and I'll always be grateful to Bobby Flay, and to this cupcake.

Makes 24 medium cupcakes

FOR CUPCAKES:

2 cups flour

1 teaspoon baking soda

3/4 teaspoon salt

2 teaspoons unsweetened cocoa powder

1 1/3 cups granulated sugar

1 cup vegetable oil

2 large eggs

1 tablespoon plus 1 teaspoon red food coloring

2 teaspoons apple cider vinegar

3/4 teaspoon vanilla

1 tablespoon plus 1 teaspoon water

1 cup plus 3 tablespoons buttermilk

Preheat oven to 325°.

Sift flour, baking soda, salt, and cocoa powder in a medium bowl. Mix well and set aside.

Using a stand mixer fitted with the paddle attachment, combine sugar, vegetable oil, eggs, red food coloring, apple cider vinegar, vanilla, and water in bowl and mix until smooth. Add flour mixture. As flour mixture incorporates, pour in buttermilk. Scrape down sides of bowl and mix until smooth.

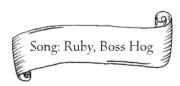

Song: Ruby, Boss Hog

Line cupcake pan with liners and scoop 1/4 cup batter into each dish. A 1 1/2-ounce to 2-ounce ice cream scoop works very well. Bake for 18 to 22 minutes, rotating the pans halfway through. Cupcakes are done when the tops are springy to the touch and a toothpick comes out clean. Let cool 10 minutes before removing from pan. Set on a cooling rack until completely cool, an additional 40 to 50 minutes. If you're in a hurry, let cupcakes cool on the rack for 10 minutes before placing them in the refrigerator for an additional 15 to 20 minutes. It is important that they cool completely or the frosting will slide off the tops.

FOR CREAM CHEESE FROSTING:

4 cups powdered sugar

1 cup unsalted butter, at room temperature

1 1/2 teaspoons vanilla extract

14 ounces cream cheese, at room temperature

Sift powdered sugar into a medium bowl. Set aside.

Using a stand mixer fitted with the paddle attachment, beat butter and vanilla on medium speed until creamy. Add cream cheese and mix on medium-low until smooth but not airy. Reduce mixer to low and add powdered sugar 1 cup at a time. Scrape down sides of bowl with a rubber spatula between cups of sugar. Mix on low speed until smooth. Refrigerate until firm enough to use, generally 30 to 40 minutes. If you are in a hurry, pour finished frosting into a flat cake pan lined with plastic wrap and place in the freezer. Be careful— this can freeze the frosting pretty quickly.

When cupcakes are cool and frosting has set, scoop 3 to 4 tablespoons, depending on your preferred cake-to-frosting ratio, onto each cupcake. Use a small offset spatula or butter knife to spread and smooth the frosting. If you're feeling adventurous, use the spatula to create a swirled design. Top with red sprinkles.

TIP:

Make the frosting the night before, so it has time to set before you frost the cupcakes.

Red Velvet Cupcake

Caramel Apple Pie

CARAMEL APPLE PIE

This pie tastes like those caramel apples on a stick that you get at the county fair. Michelle Risucci, our former head baker, dreamed this up when we had extra caramel from another dessert as well as a lot of apples. So she combined the best of both worlds inside one pie crust. It's such a winner.

Makes 1 9-inch pie

Song: Ooh La La, The Faces

FOR CARAMEL SAUCE:
1 cup granulated sugar
1 tablespoon light corn syrup
6 tablespoons water
2 tablespoons unsalted butter, room temperature
1/4 cup plus 2 tablespoons heavy cream, at room temperature
1/4 teaspoon kosher salt

In a small, heavy-bottomed saucepan, combine sugar, corn syrup, and water over medium-high heat. Dip a pastry brush in water and wipe any sugar crystals that accumulate on sides of pan back into sugar mixture, but do not stir. If sugar begins to boil or color unevenly, gently swirl the saucepan. When sugar mixture is dark golden brown, remove saucepan from the heat. Wearing an oven mitt, immediately whisk butter, cream, and salt into the sugar until smooth (be careful, the mixture will steam vigorously). Set aside to cool.

FOR CRUMB TOPPING:
1 cup flour
1/2 cup light brown sugar
3 tablespoons old-fashioned oats
8 tablespoons cold unsalted butter, cubed

Combine flour, brown sugar, and oats in a medium bowl. Mix well. Use your fingertips to crumble butter into dry ingredients. Do not overmix; there should be pea-size chunks of butter. Refrigerate while assembling the pie.

The Auntie Em's Cookbook

ASSEMBLING THE PIE:

2 pounds Granny Smith apples

1 tablespoon cornstarch

1 tablespoon lemon juice

3/4 cup plus 1/3 cup Caramel Sauce, divided

1 Cream Cheese Pie Dough (*see recipe page 194*)

Preheat oven to 400°.

Peel, core, and cut apples into 3/4-inch slices. In a medium bowl, combine apples, cornstarch, lemon juice, and 3/4 cup Caramel Sauce. Mix well; apple slices should be evenly coated with cornstarch mixture. Mound apples and any accumulated juices into prepared pie shell. Rearrange apples as needed so fruit is compactly arranged in shell and cover with Crumb Topping. Bake until topping is dark golden brown, juices are bubbling, and a toothpick stuck in the top meets little to no resistance. This usually takes from 1 hour and 15 minutes to 1 hour and 30 minutes. If edges of crust begin to brown early, cover loosely with aluminum foil (do not cover entire pie; it will make crumb topping soggy).

Cool for 15 minutes, then drizzle the top with remaining Caramel Sauce (about 1/3 cup). Serve warm, but let set for 15 more minutes after drizzling with caramel before cutting.

PEACH & PLUOT PIE

There is nothing like the aroma of a just-picked peach at the beginning of summer. Each variety has a short time with us, and you can taste the difference in each and every one. At the farmers' market, ask to taste the varieties. For years, I've been buying all my stone fruit from the same farmer, Kurt Kessler of K and K Farms, who I first met at the Hollywood Farmers' Market. Kurt cuts up slices of all his fruit to taste and gives you a little history on each one you try. He gets so excited when the white peaches ripen—he can't wait for me to taste them. When I first met Kurt, I asked if he ever got sick of peaches. "Nope," he said. Same for me.

When making baked goods, desserts, and preserves with quality fresh peaches, you need very little sugar, because they're so sweet. So this pie goes relatively easy on the sugar. I like to serve it with a dollop of Vanilla Bean Whipped Cream, which you'll find on page 195.

2 pieces Cream Cheese Pie Dough (*see recipe page 194*)

4 tablespoons unsalted butter, melted

4 medium peaches

6 medium pluots

4 tablespoons cornstarch

4 tablespoons orange juice

1/4 cup brown sugar

1/4 cup white sugar

1 large egg, beaten

Song: Peaches, The Stranglers

On a lightly floured work surface, roll out 1 piece of pie dough into a 12-inch circle. Place in 9-inch pie pan. Leave any dough that hangs over lip of pan. Roll out second piece of pie dough into an 1-inch circle. Place on a flat cookie sheet and refrigerate, along with dough in pie pan, for at least 30 minutes. After 15 minutes, brush bottom of dough in pie pan and one side of the flat piece with melted butter. Return to refrigerator. While pie dough is chilling, prepare filling.

Preheat oven to 400°.

Cut peaches and pluots into 1/2-inch slices. In a medium bowl, combine fruit, cornstarch, orange juice, and both sugars. Toss to evenly coat fruit.

Pour fruit mixture into pie pan. Place flat piece of dough butter side down on top of fruit. Pinch together dough that hangs over pie pan and top crust. Trim overhanging dough so it is no longer than 1 inch. Roll the edge under itself to create a cylinder sitting on the lip of pie pan. Using the pointer finger of one hand, press the dough between the thumb and forefinger of the other hand to create a V shape. Continue around the edge of the pie until the entire crust is crimped. Brush top of crust with a thin coat of beaten egg. Cut 3 to 6 slits in the top crust.

Bake until the crust is an even brown and the filling is bubbling, about 1 to 1 1/2 hours. If edge of the crust gets too brown before the filling bubbles, cover with a ring of aluminum foil. Do not cover the entire pie with foil as this will make the top crust soggy.

Let cool at least 1 hour before slicing.

SHAKER LEMON PIE

If you like marmalade, you will love this pie. The filling is sour-sweet, with the consistency of marmalade. It gets its name from the Shaker community, which developed the recipe at the turn of the twentieth century.

Take note that you have to start your preparation of this pie a day in advance.

Makes 1 9-inch pie

4 large lemons
3 cups sugar
1 Cream Cheese Pie Dough (*see recipe page 194*)
1/8 teaspoon sea salt
7 large eggs
1 egg white

Wash and cut 2 lemons crosswise into very thin slices. It is important for the slices to be as thin as possible, so use a sharp knife or mandoline. Remove seeds and discard. Transfer slices to a medium bowl. Remove peel and pith from a third lemon, and slice the lemon flesh crosswise into thin slices. Remove seeds and add lemon to the bowl with the other slices. Add sugar and toss well to coat. Cover bowl with plastic wrap and let mixture stand in the refrigerator for 12 hours or overnight, mixing occasionally.

Preheat the oven to 325°.

On a lightly floured work surface, roll out pie dough into a 12-inch circle and place in a 9-inch pie pan. Roll up excess dough into a cylinder atop edge of the pan. Using one finger, press the dough between the thumb and forefinger of the other hand, forming a "V" shape. Continue crimping around the edge of the pie. Refrigerate for at least 1 hour.

Pour lemon-sugar mixture into a large bowl. Add salt and eggs and stir until well combined. Pour into chilled pie crust. Slice remaining lemon into paper-thin slices, removing any seeds. Arrange slices on top of the filling. Discard or compost any remaining slices.

Bake pie until filling is firm on top and crust is golden brown, 1 to 1 1/4 hours. Filling will still jiggle. Let cool at least 1 hour before slicing.

The Auntie Em's Cookbook

Song: Spellbound, Siouxsie & the Banshees

Staples

How I Scramble Eggs

I have to say, perfectly scrambled eggs are my favorite way to eat eggs—especially on a piece of toast. Here's how I make them:

Melt 1 tablespoon butter in a heavy, shallow pan over medium heat. Break 3 eggs into a bowl, beat lightly, and tip into melted butter. Turn heat down to low and stir eggs constantly with a wooden spoon until set, about 3 to 4 minutes. Add 2 tablespoons cream, a pinch of sea salt, and freshly ground pepper, and cook about 30 seconds more, stirring constantly, until firm but still soft. Serve immediately.

How I Fry Eggs

Break an egg into a small ramekin and have it at the ready. (This make it easier to slide them into the pan without breaking.) If you're frying several eggs, have them standing by.

Heat a nonstick skillet over medium heat for a minute or so, just until the pan is warm. Add 1 tablespoon butter. When butter is melted and bubbling, slide in the egg in the ramekin. Add a second egg if you're cooking two at once. If you like your eggs cooked hard, put a lid on the pan for about 30 seconds. I like this method better than turning them with a spatula because there is less risk of breaking the yolks. Sprinkle the eggs with sea salt and freshly ground pepper, and gently take them out of the pan with a spatula. Repeat as needed.

HOW I POACH EGGS

Here's how I poach 4 eggs. Fill a wide, deep pan with about 4 inches of water and place over high heat. Add 1 teaspoon apple cider vinegar and a pinch of sea salt. Bring to a boil, reduce to medium heat, and keep at a gentle boil.

Break 1 egg at a time into a small ramekin. Tip egg into gently boiling water. Repeat with other 3 eggs. Poach for about 1 1/2 minutes for a runny yolk. Using a slotted spoon, lift out first egg and gently press outside edge of yolk to test if it is properly cooked. When eggs are cooked to your liking, remove from water with slotted spoon. Rest slotted spoon with egg on a paper towel for a few seconds to dry. Repeat with the remaining eggs.

WARM TOMATILLO SALSA

For a spicier salsa, leave seeds in the chiles. For a milder salsa, de-seed them. You can save the leftovers in an airtight container in the fridge for up to a week to heat up to serve later, or just use it cold. It's delicious either way.

Makes about 2 cups

1 pound fresh tomatillos, husks removed and washed with warm water

1 jalapeño, seeded to taste and roughly chopped

1 Serrano chile, seeded to taste and roughly chopped

2 cloves garlic, peeled

1/2 yellow onion, roughly chopped

2 tablespoons extra-virgin olive oil

1/2 teaspoon sea salt, more to taste

1/2 cup chicken or vegetable stock, preferably homemade

1/3 cup cilantro, roughly chopped

1 tablespoon freshly squeezed lime juice, more to taste

Preheat oven to 400°. Place oven rack in top third of oven.

Place tomatillos, chilies, garlic, and onions in an ovenproof glass or ceramic baking dish. Drizzle vegetables with olive oil and sprinkle with sea salt.

Roast vegetables until soft and edges start to crisp up and turn dark brown, about 20 minutes. Remove from oven, pour in stock, and deglaze pan by scraping all the sticky brown bits with a spatula. Allow to cool for a few minutes. Pour into a food processor or blender and pulse until salsa is blended but still chunky.

Pour salsa into a medium bowl and add cilantro and lime juice. Season with additional lime juice and salt to taste. Serve warm.

CILANTRO PESTO

I serve this with the crab cakes on page 30, but it's good on so many things—experiment!

Makes 1 cup

3 cloves garlic, peeled and roughly chopped

2 cups fresh cilantro, lightly packed

1/4 cup extra-virgin olive oil

2 tablespoons freshly squeezed lemon juice

1/2 teaspoon sea salt, more to taste

1/2 teaspoon freshly ground pepper,
more to taste

Place garlic and cilantro in food processor. With processor running, slowly drizzle in oil and lemon juice until smooth. Add salt and pepper, taste, and add more if desired. Refrigerate for up to 4 days.

APPLE CIDER VINAIGRETTE

An essential staple in every kitchen. Put a damp dish towel under your bowl while whisking to keep it steady.

Makes 1 cup

1/4 cup apple cider vinegar

2 tablespoons Dijon mustard

1 clove garlic, minced

2 teaspoons sea salt

1 teaspoon freshly ground pepper

2/3 cup extra-virgin olive oil

Place vinegar, mustard, garlic, salt, and pepper in a medium bowl. Whisk to incorporate. Slowly drizzle in oil, whisking constantly, until emulsified. Store in a jar and refrigerate for up to 1 week.

CHIPOTLE AIOLI

This is a super-simple recipe that adds a ton of flavor to any egg dish. It's one of my most essential go-to condiments.

1 cup good-quality mayonnaise

1 chipotle pepper (canned)

1 teaspoon adobo sauce (canned)

Juice of 1/2 lemon

In a food processor, combine mayonnaise, chipotle, and adobo sauce. Blend for 30 seconds, scrape down the edges, and add lemon juice. Blend for 30 more seconds. Store in a clean jar and refrigerate for up to 4 days.

CREAM CHEESE PIE DOUGH

Because it's a plain dough, this can be used for anything, sweet or savory. Some pies in the book are single-crust and some are double-crust, which is why the recipe makes three pieces—enough for one double-crust and one single-crust, or extra for your freezer.

Makes 3 pieces

3 cups flour
1/4 teaspoon sea salt
1/2 teaspoon baking powder
6 ounces (3/4 cup) cream cheese, cut into 1-inch pieces
8 ounces (2 sticks) unsalted butter, cut into 1-inch pieces
1 tablespoon plus 1 teaspoon apple cider vinegar
2 to 4 tablespoons ice water, divided

In a medium bowl, sift together flour, salt, and baking powder. Using a pastry cutter or your fingertips, cut cream cheese into flour mixture until the largest pieces are pea size. Repeat with butter.

Sprinkle apple cider vinegar and 1 tablespoon ice water over bowl and mix to combine. Add remaining water 1 tablespoon at a time, just until the dough begins to stick together. Do not overmix—dough should be relatively dry with some streaks of butter. Divide dough into 3 pieces. Shape each into 4-inch by 1-inch disks and wrap in plastic. Refrigerate at least 2 hours before using. The dough will keep in the freezer for a month.

This recipe uses only the seeds of a vanilla bean. Save the outside for a recipe that steeps a vanilla bean, or put it in a container of powdered sugar to make vanilla sugar.

Makes 2 cups

1 cup heavy cream, more as needed
1 whole vanilla bean
3 tablespoons powdered sugar, more to taste

Place cream in bowl of a stand mixer fitted with the whisk attachment. Cut vanilla bean lengthwise and scrape out seeds with a paring knife. Try not to scrape off any of the fibrous bean husk. Add seeds and powdered sugar to bowl and mix on low speed until sugar and vanilla are well incorporated, about 30 seconds. Taste and add more powdered sugar if desired. On high speed, whip cream until it doubles in size and holds its shape. For softer whipped cream, this takes about 3 to 4 minutes; for firmer whipped cream, whip a minute longer. If cream becomes over-whipped and begins to look like butter, turn mixer to low and add additional cream 1 tablespoon at a time until it reaches desired consistency. If necessary, add additional powdered sugar to balance any added cream.

BRIOCHE DOUGH

This is the master recipe for the cinnamon sugar–infused dough for Auntie Em's Cinnamon Rolls, Sticky Buns, and Monkey Bread. Each calls for 1 brioche dough recipe. It's great to keep handy in the freezer.

FOR DOUGH:

2 2/3 cups flour
1 1/4 teaspoons sea salt
3 large eggs
1/4 cup whole milk
2 1/4 teaspoons dry active yeast
1/3 cup granulated sugar, divided
4 ounces (1 stick) unsalted butter, cut in half

Combine flour and salt in bowl of a stand mixer fitted with the paddle attachment. Break eggs into a small bowl and set aside.

In a small pot, heat milk over medium heat until scalding, or when small bubbles begin to form at edges and steam comes off the surface of the milk (it should be hot to the touch). Remove from heat and let cool to between 100° and 110°. (If you don't have a thermometer, add the yeast when milk is very warm to the touch but not hot. If milk is too warm or too cold, the yeast will not activate.) Whisk in yeast and mix until fully combined.

Immediately pour milk into flour mixture, add eggs, and mix until evenly combined. Dough will be very sticky, so scrape down paddle regularly with a rubber spatula. Cover bowl with plastic wrap and let rest for 10 minutes.

Uncover the bowl, turn mixer on low, and add half the sugar while mixer is running. Scrape down bowl and add remaining sugar. Add half the butter and mix until fully incorporated. Scrape down sides of bowl and add remaining butter. Continue to mix dough until smooth and pale in color, about 5 to 8 minutes.

Spray a large bowl with cooking spray. Pour dough into bowl and cover with plastic wrap. Let rest in a warm space until doubled in size, 1 to 1 1/2 hours, or refrigerate overnight.

The Auntie Em's Cookbook

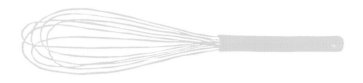

FOR CINNAMON SUGAR FILLING AND ASSEMBLY:

Flour, for dusting

1 large egg

2 tablespoons water

2 tablespoons melted butter

2 teaspoons cinnamon

1/3 cup granulated sugar

1/3 cup brown sugar

Generously flour a large, flat work surface. Use plenty of flour to keep dough from sticking to the table. Scrape dough out of bowl and roll into a lengthwise rectangle about 10 inches by 13 inches.

In a small bowl, whisk egg with water and brush lengthwise on the edge of the dough rectangle farthest away from you, in a 1-inch strip. Brush remaining dough with melted butter.

Mix the cinnamon and both sugars together in a small bowl. Sprinkle cinnamon sugar mixture over buttered portion of dough. Starting with the closest edge facing you, gently roll dough up to egg-washed portion. When you reach the edge, finish by patting down the seam. The egg wash should hold the roll together. (It's fine if some cinnamon sugar falls out the ends.) If the outside of the cinnamon roll is very sticky, pat or brush a little additional flour on the sticky parts to make more manageable. Refrigerate for 30 minutes before using. You may also wrap it tightly in plastic wrap and freeze for up to a month.

MINT ICED TEA

This elixir couldn't be simpler—it has just two ingredients, mint and water. We've served it at Auntie Em's since we opened, and it's always been popular. It's a really refreshing drink on a hot day.

Makes 1/2 gallon

1/2 gallon water
6 sprigs organic mint

Bring water to a boil in a medium pot. Turn off heat, add mint, and let steep for 20 minutes. Strain mint and cool tea completely. Serve over ice, and sweeten if desired. Keep in a covered pitcher in the refrigerator for up to a week.

RASPBERRY LEMONADE

We sell a lot of raspberry lemonade. A lot.

Makes about 3/4 gallon

1 cup sugar, more to taste
1 cup hot water
1 cup freshly squeezed lemon juice (about 8 lemons)
1/2 gallon cold water
1 cup fresh raspberries

In a large, heat-proof pitcher, combine sugar and hot water. Stir until sugar is dissolved. Add lemon juice, cold water, and raspberries. Mix well. Taste and add more sugar and hot water if it's too tart.

Set aside for 1 hour before serving so raspberries release their juice. Serve over ice. Keep in a covered pitcher in the refrigerator for up to a week.

A Guide to the Recipes

What's Vegetarian?

What's Vegan?

Apple Cider Vinaigrette, 54
Asparagus with Gremolata, 40
Beet & Blood Orange Salad, 123
Bread & Butter Pickles, 78
Cilantro Pesto, 192
Cranberry Beans with Black Kale & Red Chiles, 124
Curried Chickpea Salad, 115
Dilly Beans, 81
Double Garlic Greens, 113
Green Tomato & Zucchini Chow Chow, 86
Indian Spiced Roasted Carrots, 42
Laura Ann's Blueberry Basil Jam, 88

Mint Iced Tea, 199
Oven-dried Tomatoes in Olive Oil, 84
Pear & Cranberry Compote, 116
Quick Heirloom Tomato Sauce, 82
Raspberry Lemonade, 199
Refrigerator Pickles, 79
Rhubarb Compote, 41
Spicy Ketchup, 85
Spicy Melon & Peanut Salad, 50
Spicy Pickled Beets, 80

What's Gluten-Free?

Andouille Sausage & Shrimp Scramble, 101
Apple Cider Vinaigrette, 54
Artichoke Baked Eggs*, 33
Asparagus with Gremolata, 40
Baked Eggs in Ham Baskets, 133
Baked Eggs in Spicy Tomato Sauce, 68
Basil Pesto, 89
Beet & Blood Orange Salad, 123
Best Cobb Ever, 54
Braised Pork with Greens & Eggs, 106
Bread & Butter Pickles, 78
Brussels Sprouts & Potato Hash with Poached
   Eggs, 111
Chipotle Aioli, 193
Cilantro Pesto, 192
Crab Cakes & Eggs with Chipotle Aioli & Cilantro
   Pesto, 30
Crabby Deviled Eggs, 34
Cranberry Beans with Black Kale & Red Chiles, 124
Curried Chickpea Salad, 115
Dilly Beans, 81
Fennel, Tomato & Parmesan Salad with Poached
   Eggs, 103
Granola & Yogurt Parfait, 56
Green Tomato & Zucchini Chow Chow, 86
Heirloom Bean & Tomato Salad, 53
Herb-roasted Breakfast Potatoes, 112
Laura Ann's Blueberry Basil Jam, 88

Mint Iced Tea, 199
Oven-dried Tomatoes in Olive Oil, 84
Peach, Burrata, Prosciutto & Hazelnut Salad, 48
Pear & Cranberry Compote, 116
Quick Heirloom Tomato Sauce, 82
Raspberry Lemonade, 199
Refrigerator Pickles, 79
Rhubarb Compote, 41
Roasted Mushroom Grits & Poached Eggs, 108
Salmon & Fennel Scramble with Dill Crème
   Fraîche, 134
Spicy Ketchup, 85
Spicy Melon & Peanut Salad, 50
Spicy Pickled Beets, 80
Spicy Sausage & Cheddar Grits, 136
Swiss Chard Gratin, 141
Tomato & Goat Cheese Frittata, 63
Tomato & Onion Provençal*, 71
Tomato & Spinach Frittata with Green Tomato
   Chow Chow, 65
Vanilla Bean Whipped Cream, 195
Vegetarian Red Flannel Hash, 36
Wilted Spinach & Lentil Salad with Poached
   Eggs, 130
Zucchini & Potato Hash Browns with Poached
   Eggs & Sweet 100 Tomatoes, 66

* *Gluten-free if you substitute crushed rice crisps or
   similar for the breadcrumbs*

Kitchen Playlists

Here are my playlists by chapter, to get you started. I hope you discover a few new favorite songs to add to your own kitchen playlists. It's always more fun to cook to music—I love it as much as I used to love playing with The Red Aunts!

Spring
Tive Razao, Seu Jorge
Home Grown, Booker T. & the M.G.'s
Beautiful Gardens, The Cramps
The Day My Baby Gave Me a Surprise, Devo
Superfly, Curtis Mayfield
Crabdance, The Gun Club
Eggs on My Plate, Iggy Pop
All You Can Eat, Fat Boys
Flavor, Jon Spencer Blues Explosion
Feelin' Good, Jessie Mae Hemphill
Little Friend, The Ponys
Gatecrasher, Dan Melchior's Broke Revue
Imaginary Person, Ty Segall

Summer
Peach Kelli Pop, Redd Kross
Hot Pants, James Brown
Little Olive, The Electric Prunes
Here Comes the Summer, The Undertones
Summertime Blues, Blue Cheer
Pleasure, Girls at Our Best!
Pancakes, Mark Sultan
California Paradise, The Runaways
In the Sun, Blondie
Sunny Afternoon, The Kinks
Sunshine Girl, The Dirtbombs
Hang a Picture, Thee Oh Sees
Mater Dolores, The Screamers
Dancing Days, Led Zeppelin

Preserving the End of Summer
Come on in My Kitchen, Robert Johnson
All Your Love, Otis Rush
Knocked Out Cold, Action Swingers
Something's Got a Hold of Me, Etta James
Sugar Sugar, Jimmy Reed
Bourgeois Blues, Lead Belly
Brown Sugar, The Rolling Stones
Jelly Roll Blues, Jelly Roll Morton
C Jam Blues, Duke Ellington
Pretty Thing, Bo Diddley

Fall
Real Smiles, White Fence
Thrill of it All, Roxy Music
I'm Blue, The Shangri-Las
Satisfy You, The Seeds
Live Wire, The Meters
Salad Days, Minor Threat
The Swag, Link Wray
I Want You, The Troggs
Girls Ain't Groceries, Little Milton
Red Hot Mama, Parliament
Potato, Tyvek
Just Right, Beasts of Bourbon
Highly Inflammable, X-Ray Spex
Outdoor Miner, Wire

Winter
The Witch, The Sonics
You Got Me Floatin', The Jimi Hendrix Experiment
Give Me the Cure, Fugazi
Chocolate Jesus, Tom Waits
Ugly Breakfast, Salamander Jim
Winter, The Rolling Stones
Frying Pan, Captain Beefheart & the Magic Band
Kielbasa, Tenacious D
In Heaven, Peter Ivers
Pass the Biscuits, Please, Andre Williams
It's a Rainy Day, Sunshine Girl, Faust

Desserts & Baked Goods
Lucky Monkeys, Iggy Pop & James Williamson
Sticky and Sweet, Cows
Cinnamon Girl, Neil Young
Baby Lemonade, Syd Barrett
Dyna-mite, Mud
Blues for My Cookie, Lightnin' Hopkins
Looking for a Kiss, New York Dolls
Higher Ground, Red Hot Chili Peppers
The Wild One, Suzi Quatro
Blockbuster, Sweet
Chocolate River, The Seeds
Pink Pussycat, Devo
The Coconut, Thee Oh Sees
Green Fuz, The Cramps
Gudbuy T' Jane, Slade
Ruby, Boss Hog
Ooh La La, The Faces
Peaches, The Stranglers
Spellbound, Siouxsie & the Banshees

Thanks to:

My customers! Without you I could not live my dream of cooking for a living.

My mom, my dad, and my sister, Lisa Chavers, who have always encouraged my creativity, competitiveness, and crazy ideas.

Charles Hart, for always being able to calm me down, being my anchor, encouraging me without harping, making me laugh all the time, and building a new coop for the girls.

Editor Colleen Dunn Bates, for taking a chance on putting out a "punk rock" cookbook, gently nudging me to get the book done, and always being so incredibly positive, encouraging, and optimistic.

The rest of the team at Prospect Park Books—Jennifer Bastien, Patty O'Sullivan, and Renee Nakagawa—for helping to make this book a reality and for introducing it to the world.

Talya Mirkin and Trisha Cole of Wagstaff, for all the love you show us at Auntie Em's.

My band, The Red Aunts—Kerry Davis, Debi Martini, and Lesley Ishino—for giving me the experience of a lifetime!!!! We rocked hard!

Larry Hardy, for being my best friend and music guru.

Jimmy Hole, for teaching me to play Red Aunts' songs and for being such a good friend for the last twenty years.

Noah Wolf, for always having my back at Auntie Em's and contributing in such a creative way to the menu.

Donna Coppola, for being rock solid year after year, and for being such a giant part of Auntie Em's since the beginning. Your dedication keeps me going.

Jeff Howell, for taking charge at Auntie Em's, always having the restaurant's best interests at heart, and always laughing at my jokes, even when they're not funny.

Jenn Garbee, for recipe editing and catching the tiniest of errors.

Amy Paliwoda, for styling the photos so beautifully and for at least indulging my ideas, even though you knew they were a little far-fetched.

David Kiang, for taking absolutely stunning photos and for being so patient!

Amy Inouye, for the gorgeous design and layout.

Annika Huston, for the beautiful wood block prints in the cookbook, your enthusiasm for Auntie Em's, and your endless creativity!

Michelle Risucci, for managing the zoo at Auntie Em's. I couldn't do it without you! Thanks for dotting my i's and crossing my t's.

Arlene Gonzalez, for preparing such lovely food for our catering customers.

Cristine Spindler, for making the world a more beautiful place with your smile and attitude. You treat every customer as if they are your friend.

Tommy Branch, for being with me at Auntie Em's for sooooooo long. You were one of my first employees!

Elayne Sawaya, for being a catering manager extraordinaire!

Maria Stabile, for helping me refine these recipes.

Amanda Haas, for being the amazing baker you are and for being the go-to person for adapting the baking recipes for the home cook.

TaggeeLee Mermis Bowers, for your careful recipe testing.

Debi Martini, for your super-helpful recipe testing.

Nicole Policicchio, for testing recipes and checking for their vegan-ness.

David and Maritte Hart, for painstakingly testing (and eating) so many dishes. Your notes were invaluable.

Josh Klinghoffer, Kate Schellenbach, Jack Black, and Mark Haskell Smith, for saying such nice things about me and the food at Auntie Em's.

All of my inspiring employees now and in years past. "Always surround yourself with people who are smarter and more creative than you" has worked out well for me!

INDEX

The Auntie Em's Cookbook